COMMON
PRAYER

POCKET EDITION

COMMON PRAYER

POCKET EDITION

A LITURGY
FOR ORDINARY RADICALS

SHANE CLAIBORNE
JONATHAN WILSON-HARTGROVE

ZONDERVAN.com/
AUTHORTRACKER
follow your favorite authors

ZONDERVAN

Common Prayer Pocket Edition
Copyright © 2012 by The Simple Way and School for Conversion

This title is also available as a Zondervan ebook. Visit www.zondervan.com/ebooks.

This title is also available in a Zondervan audio edition. Visit www.zondervan.fm.

Requests for information should be addressed to:

Zondervan, *Grand Rapids, Michigan* 49530

ISBN 978-0-310-33506-1

Published in association with the literary agency of Daniel Literary Group, LLC, 1701 Kingsbury Drive, Suite 100, Nashville, TN 37215.

Woodblock prints for February, July, October, and December are by Rick Beerhorst (www.studiobeerhorst.com).

Linoleum block prints for January, March, April, May, June, August, September, and November are by Joel Klepac (www.joelklepac.com).

Woodblock prints for Evening, Morning, and Midday are by Jesce Walz (www.jesce.net).

Cover image: Shutterstock®
Interior design: Beth Shagene

Printed in the United States of America

23 24 25 26 27 LBC 20 19 18 17 16

CV 12 18 2023 0240

If someone's work takes them so far away that they cannot return to the chapel for common prayer, they should pray the office where they are, and kneel out of reverence for God.... The same goes for members who are traveling away from the community: they should keep the offices as best they can, not neglecting their measure of service.

— Benedict of Nursia (RB 50)

CONTENTS

A NOTE ABOUT THE POCKET EDITION

Common Prayer Pocket Edition was created as part of a larger project aimed at uniting people around the world in prayer and action. This book is not meant to replace the original six-hundred-page prayer book; it's meant to complement it. It is based on the same content and rhythm as the larger volume but has been abbreviated so it travels well. It's like backup vocals. Or like the French horn, which evidently goes really well with the rest of the orchestra but doesn't have the same flair when it stands on its own. We want to encourage you as you use this edition to connect with the larger liturgy whenever you are able.

One of the aims of *Common Prayer* was to remind one another that we are not alone in the world. As we pray and as we act, we are participating in a beautiful redemptive love story. So as you use the pocket edition, even though it works well for individuals who are on the go, remember that there are folks around the world praying these same prayers with you.

We also anticipate this little version will open up some new possibilities that may be trickier with a big ole six-hundred-page book, like being able to take it to class or to work or on your bike or on a hike with a few friends. Or it may happen that you randomly connect with someone else who is a "pocket pray-er" and get the chance to do midday prayer together in a park somewhere. Keep your eyes open for opportunities and surprises.

There are a few things to note as you begin using the pocket edition.

Daily Prayer: one reason the original edition is so large is that it contains unique prayers for each morning of the year. For the sake of space, we did things a little differently here. As in the original edition, we have morning, midday, and evening prayers (or offices); to more fully round out the daily cycle, we have added a compline office. And instead of providing unique prayers for the morning and evening offices, these offices are the same — with the exception of the daily Scripture readings — every day.

One of our unique contributions to historic liturgy is integrating the church calendar with the world calendar in order to situate our prayer lives in the real world, or as Karl Barth said, "To hold the Bible in one hand and the newspaper in the other." For this reason, we have created a table so that you can easily find the Scripture readings and dates commemorating saints and historic events for each day of the year. And we have compiled an annotated list of these special days from the original edition so you can walk with them daily as you pray.

Additions and Omissions: We had to do some tinkering to stay true to the "pocket" part of this edition. We shortened and modified the introduction. (The acknowledgments are the same, though, by the way.) We left out the songs ... had to. The larger edition has dozens of the "greatest hits" from church history, and you can consult that edition or the audio version or check the website *www.commonprayer.net.* We also left out the sidebar reflections on prayer and ideas for a more robust life of prayer and action. We have kept the twelve monthly reflections on contemporary practices of the Christian life. These "twelve marks of new monasticism" are the core holy habits we hope to cultivate in our lives and in our communities. And finally, though we shortened the occasional prayers section, we did add a few prayers to make it richer for when traveling or when praying alone.

When we set out on this adventure years ago, we had a deep sense that the Spirit was up to something wonderful. And that has only been confirmed as a movement has stirred around the world. When we released the original edition, folks threw prayer parties all over the world. We heard stories of old and young coming together, charismatic evangelicals and mainliners, folks from all walks of life and of all colors of skin. We've had families that had never known how to pray together tell us they now have a tool, and folks in prison and in retirement homes tell us they use it there. We heard stories of Protestants and Catholics in Northern Ireland coming together, and folks in suburban cul-de-sacs gathering each day with *Common Prayer*. And something beautiful continues to happen. It has truly felt like a sacred endeavor. We trust that *Common Prayer Pocket Edition* will be a fruitful gift to you, so that you can be a fruitful gift to the world.

INTRODUCTION

There are so many divisions within Christianity. By one count, there are more than thirty-eight thousand Christian denominations. Many people have said that the greatest barrier to becoming a Christian is all the division they see in the church.

God's deepest longing is for the church to be united as one body. In Jesus' longest recorded prayer, he prayed that we would be "one as God is one." As one old preacher said, "We gotta get it together, because Jesus is coming back, and he's coming for a bride, not a harem."

God has only one church.

This prayer book is the result of a collaboration of people from many different branches of Christianity, all of which come from one trunk — if you trace the branches all the way back.

Folks are bound to ask if this prayer book is for Catholics or for Protestants. Our answer is, "Yes, it is." We want the fire of the Pentecostals, the imagination of the Mennonites, the Lutherans' love of Scripture, the Benedictines' discipline, the wonder of the Catholics and the Orthodox. We've drawn on some of the oldest and richest traditions of Christian prayer. And we've tried to make them dance.

Our prayer lives connect us to the rest of the body of Christ around the world; at any hour of any day, many of the prayers in this book are being prayed in some corner of the earth. Using these prayers is also a way of connecting ourselves to the past; we're talking about the greatest hits not just from the 1960s, '70s, and '80s but from the 1800s and the 300s. Some of these prayers are more than a thousand years old.

A Word about Liturgy

Liturgy comes from the Greek word *leitourgia*, meaning "public worship." When we hear the phrase *public worship*, many of us think of large meetings, like Sunday morning services, and while public worship *can* mean that, it doesn't have to take place in a big group. After all, *public* shares the same root word as *pub*, and it really just refers to a gathering of people to share life (and maybe a drink), a get-together that's always open to strangers joining in. Jesus promised that wherever two or three gather in his name, he'll be there with us. Jesus will be with us at the "pub," whether there's wine or not.

When we first experience the organized cycle of readings that is a part of liturgical worship — a lectionary, as it's often called — it can seem like magic or a conspiracy. We may hear a pastor preach from the same text we read in morning prayer and think, "How in the world? The Spirit must be moving!" And, in fact, the Spirit is moving, just in a more organized way than we would have guessed. Some liturgical types smile when evangelicals discover the "miracle" of the liturgy. But it is a miracle nonetheless. So lean in and listen as you pray these prayers. Sometimes it may feel like you can hear the church's heart beat as you pray in a way you never have before.

The readings of the church are arranged in a three-year cycle so that we hear the entire biblical story — creation and fall, the exodus, captivity and return, the promise and advent of the Messiah, the coming of the Holy Spirit, and the promise of the coming kingdom. This cycle is used all over the world, so that on the same day, Christians in Africa are reading the same texts as Christians in Latin America. Since *Common Prayer* is designed to be used year after year, we have done our best to honor this cycle, though we've squeezed it into one year.

Participating in the liturgy of the worldwide Christian community, whether on a Sunday morning or at another time, is more than attending a service or a prayer meeting. It is about entering a story. It is about orienting our lives around what God has been doing throughout history. And it is about being sent forth into the world to help write the next chapter of that story.

Liturgy offers us an invitation not just to observe but to participate — active prayer, active worship. "Peace be with you" invites us to respond, "And also with you." When we hear "God is good," we want to call back, "All the time." It is a dialogue, a divine drama in which we are the actors. We become a part of God's story. We sing God's songs. We discover lost ancestors. And their story becomes our story.

Welcome to a Whole New World

Liturgy invites us to see the reality of the universe through a new lens. It helps us to see ourselves as part of a holy counterculture, a people being "set apart" from the world around us (and the world inside us) to bear witness that another world is possible. We're invited to become a peculiar people, living into a different story and orienting our lives around a different set of values than those we are taught by the empires and markets around us. In an individualistic culture, liturgy helps us live a communal life. In an everchanging world, liturgy roots us in the eternal — a God who is the same yesterday and today and tomorrow, no matter what happens on Wall Street.

Liturgy's counterintuitive nature may feel a little strange at first. It is weird enough in our culture just to get together to sing songs (unless you are going to a concert or playing Rock Band on the Wii). Singing and praying together can feel awkward, especially if it is not Thanksgiving or Christmas. But liturgy is meant to be an interruption. It disrupts our reality and refocuses it on God. It reshapes our perceptions and lives with new rhythms, new holy days, a whole new story.

What we discover is not just a poetic genius behind the words but a community in, with, and under the words. Just as people of the world pledge allegiance to flags or sing national anthems with pride and adoration, these creeds, songs, and prayers are ways that we proclaim our allegiance and sing our adoration not to a nation but to another kingdom altogether. That may sound a little esoteric or ethereal, like heaven is less real than the stuff of earth. But liturgy actually draws us out of the world of counterfeit power and splendor and into something *more* real. As we pray, the world of billboards and neon signs and false promises becomes ghostlike. We are invited into an ancient and eternal place and time that transcends all that is around us.

Welcome to a New Time Zone

Every sturdy society has created its own calendar according to its own values. For some time now, Western civilization has used the Julian and Gregorian calendars, which are influenced largely by the Roman Empire's traditions. The United States' civil religion uses this calendar, mixing in its own set of holy days, most notably its date of inception (the Fourth of July) and its remembrances of human sacrifice (Memorial Day and Veterans Day). Consumer culture always threatens to monopolize the feast days on which the church remembers saints like Nicholas, Valentine, and Patrick, turning them into little more than days to buy stuff in the name of cultural idols such as Santa, the Easter bunny, and green leprechauns. Too often we have forgotten the lives of the people for whom these days are named.

But if we are going to take our citizenship in heaven seriously, we must mark our calendars differently. We must observe the holidays of the biblical narrative rather than the festivals of the Caesars, and celebrate feast days that remember saints rather than war heroes and presidents. And instead of commemorating people who sacrificed themselves in order to kill for their country, we find a deeper and more powerful observance on Good Friday, when we remember that Jesus willingly died for everyone in the world, even his enemies, instead of killing them to "change the world."

We enter a new time zone, where it can feel like there is a "cloud of witnesses" surrounding us, praying for us, cheering us on from eternity. It should feel like we are singing "Holy, Holy, Holy" with all of the people of God who have come before us. The past becomes bigger than our personal pasts. God's story becomes the lens through which we understand the present. And the future is no longer held hostage. We know how the story ends, and it is beautiful. This is the good news that transcends the nightly news.

The worldwide church has its holy days, such as the Presentation, the Annunciation, the Visitation, and the Transfiguration. These are our holidays. It is not that we need a "Christian" calendar because we want to separate ourselves from the "secular" world. The point is to keep God's story at the center of our lives. We also have our own hall of fame. There are days when we highlight women and men throughout church history (often on the days they died). These people are exemplary models of Christian discipleship from around the world and across the centuries, and they're just really fascinating people who have lived well. It is our hope that their lives and courage will inspire us, and rub off on us, as they point us to Christ. In their imperfect but beautiful lives, we can see our own potential.

The daily cycle of prayer — morning, midday, evening, and compline — is like a heartbeat for the global church, passing from one time zone to the next each day, so that we as a people can, as the apostle Paul taught us, pray without ceasing. But this daily rhythm is but a "wheel within a wheel" of the weekly cycle, which begins on Sunday (Resurrection Day), remembers Jesus' gathering the twelve disciples on Thursday, suffers with Christ symbolically on Friday, and prepares on Saturday for the great feast after the resurrection. And then we do it all again, and again.

But the weekly cycle also happens within an annual rhythm of seasons — Advent to prepare for Christ's coming, Christmas to celebrate the Prince of Peace, Epiphany to remember the Light, Lent to confess our resistance to the Light, Holy Week to remember Christ's suffering, Easter to celebrate the resurrection's power, the birthday of the church at Pentecost, and Ordinary Time to bring us back to the beginning again.

The church calendar does not help us remember our appointments, but it helps us remember who we are. It aims at nothing less than changing the way we experience time and perceive reality. It is about the movement of history toward a glorious goal — God's kingdom on earth as it is in heaven.

Why *Common* Prayer?

No doubt, we can pray to God by ourselves; for centuries both monks and evangelicals (and lots of people in between) have prayed solitarily. There is something beautiful about a God who is personal, who talks face to face with Moses, wrestles with Jacob, and becomes fully human in Jesus, a God who needs no mediation, with whom we can speak as a Friend and Lover at any moment and in any place, in a cathedral or an alleyway.

The point of this book is certainly not to take away from the intimacy each of us can have with God. Personal or devotional prayer and communal prayer are not at odds with each other. In fact, they must go together. Just as God is communal, God is also deeply personal and intimate.

Certainly one of the unique and beautiful things about Jesus is his intimacy with God as he runs off to the mountaintop or hides away in the garden. Jesus daringly invites us to approach the God of the universe as Abba (Daddy) or as a mother caring for her little chicks. Our God is personal and wildly in love with each of us.

But just because our prayer lives are personal does not mean they are private. Many of us have grown up in a culture where rampant individualism has affected our prayer lives. When we think about prayer, our imaginations may be limited to evening devotions or a daily "quiet time" with God. As wonderful as these times of solitude can be, prayer moves us beyond what we can do on our own.

The gift of liturgy is that it helps us hear less of our own little voices and more of God's still, small voice (Psalm 46). It leads us away from self and points us toward the community of God. God is a plurality of oneness. God has "lived in community" from eternity as Father, Son, and Holy Spirit. God as Trinity is the core reality of the universe, and that means that the core of reality is community. We often live as if the essence of our being is the "I," and as if the "we" of community is a nice add-on or an "intentional" choice. But the truth is we are made for community — we are made in the image of community — and if we live outside of community, we are selling ourselves short.

What about When You're Not Feeling It?

Common Prayer isn't so much an inspirational text as it is a workout guide. Though it can be a little easier to exercise with others, jogging alone is still good for the body, and so is praying alone.

Liturgy is active. It takes patience (one part of the fruit of the Spirit, by the way). And patience is very countercultural. Sometimes we don't feel like working out our bodies, but after the first few steps, we start to breathe, and we can feel our heartbeat, which had grown quiet and lethargic. Liturgy is not simply about watching or listening; it's about participating. You can sit back with a bowl of popcorn and watch all the exercise videos you want, but nothing will happen until you get off the couch and start sweatin' to the oldies.

In many ways, the "official" liturgy can't work for each of us if we're not doing things to stay in shape outside of the fixed hours for prayer. Study, discipleship, works of mercy, and contemplation are the homework assignments that prepare us for the experience of worship and prayer together. Otherwise, it's like going on a jog every day but only eating junk and staring at a television the rest of the time. If we don't spend time listening for God during the day, liturgy can feel like we are being invited to laugh at a joke we haven't even heard yet. How can you enjoy the romance unless you have spent some time falling in love? If *Common Prayer* doesn't work for you right away, hang in there and give the divine romance a chance.

But also, a disclaimer: the liturgy is not a magic formula. You can have liturgy without life in it, just as you can have a nice-looking car that doesn't run. Some of the dreariest services on the planet are rich with liturgy and traditions. Liturgy is one of the most powerful places to meet and be transformed by God. It is also one of the best places to hide — from God and from others. So may it be a doorway into deeper relationship with God and with others. If it's not, may you keep knocking until you find a door that opens.

How to Use This Book

This book provides four daily prayers, or daily offices — morning, midday, evening, and compline — for use at different times during the day.

As is the case with most prayer books, the offices are designed to have one person lead. Feel free to rotate who that person is, but it is usually helpful to have one person get things rolling. Prayers in normal type are to be said by the leader; prayers in bold type can be said by everyone together. Words in italic type are headings or instructions and are not meant to be read aloud. Also, a colon

with a space before and after it (:) indicates a pause. Here's a
visual key for future reference:

> Normal type = to be read by single voice/leader
> **Bold type** = to be read by community
> *Italic type* = instructions/headings, not to be read
> A colon (:) = pause

Morning Prayer

The morning office is designed to be prayed as you wake up and
greet the day. You should be able to pray it in about a half hour.
The morning office invites participation through responsorial
prayer, Scripture readings, and songs to sing if you are praying
with others. If you are by yourself, we hope you'll hear the echoes
of others' voices and remember you are not alone.

You will need to use two other sections of the book in
conjunction with the morning office: the "Table of Scripture
Readings and Special Days," and the "Annotated List of Special
Days."

The "Table of Scripture Readings and Special Days" lists the daily
readings from the Psalms and the Old and New Testaments.
Selecting the readings was a little tricky, since the traditional
liturgy of the church follows a three-year cycle. We've done our
best to honor this cycle with selected readings. We've also tried
to honor the cycle of readings from the book of Psalms. Each
month, we move through the sequence of the one hundred and
fifty psalms, skipping quite a few, of course, but reading at least a
little bit of every psalm by the time we end the year. The Old and
New Testament readings for each day also move consecutively
through biblical books, with the occasional interruption for a
holiday with a fixed date.

In addition to the readings, the table also lists special days commemorating an event or a saint. In the "Annotated List of Special Days" section, you'll find information about these days.

For events, you'll find an "On This Day in History" type of story to remind us of significant moments in the pursuit of peace and justice over the centuries — remembrances, for example, that on this day, Nagasaki was bombed, or Rosa Parks went to jail, or Martin Luther King Jr. was killed, or Nelson Mandela was released from prison. One of the unique contributions of this prayer book is to weave into our prayer lives the ongoing struggle for peace and justice, to help us pray with the Bible in one hand and the newspaper in the other. The list of events we commemorate in this book is nowhere near exhaustive, but we did our best, with a very diverse group of friends, to identify global events, both magnificent and terrible, that have been landmark moments, especially as we pray for God's kingdom to come on earth.

For saints, you'll find notes on each so we can remember different people who have exemplified what our faith is about. Usually we recognize them on their birthdays or on the days of their deaths (which are really only another kind of birthday, especially for those who were martyred). We have been careful to celebrate the legacy both of Saints with a big *S* (people who are cannonized saints) and saints with a little *S* (people who give us glimpses of faithful discipleship).

Midday Prayer

Midday prayer is meant to carve out space in the busyness of our days to center us on Christ. It is a simple office of prayer put together from various ancient sources and monastic traditions, and can be prayed in about ten minutes. Midday prayer is a great way to gather coworkers and colleagues to be refreshed for the rest of the day. If your life prohibits you from taking a noontime break for prayer, you could try integrating elements of this office into your day, even praying in a bathroom stall if you have to.

Evening Prayer

We created the evening office in the hope that, just as the morning office allows us to greet the morning together, the evening office will allow us to retire from the day together. The office is a simple prayer you should be able to pray in fifteen to twenty minutes. The evening office focuses on confession — the confession of our sins, and the confession of our faith. And we have grafted onto the evening office some of the core creeds and scriptural songs that are hundreds and even thousands of years old.

Compline

This pocket edition of *Common Prayer* adds a new compline office to pray before going to bed at the end of the day. It's easy to memorize, and can be prayed in less than five minutes. (Though if you have trouble falling asleep, it can also serve to order an extended dialog with God.) *Compline* shares the same root as the word *complete* and refers to the final prayer for the day. In many monasteries, it is the custom to begin the "Great Silence" after compline, during which the whole community, including guests, observe silence throughout the night until morning prayer the following day. We hope you'll receive this office as a daily invitation to rest in God, trusting the love that created the heavens to keep you and watch over your place throughout the night.

Monthly Action Section

The "Monthly Action" section features a lovely piece of art, reflections on one of the twelve marks of new monasticism, and a list of suggested reading for each month. Several years ago, we held a little ecclesial council of sorts, a gathering of dozens of communities, old and young, to try to identify the DNA of the current renewal we see in the church. As we tried to listen to the Spirit together, twelve distinctive marks of that renewal jumped out at us. As we worked on this book, those twelve marks seemed to flow well with the months of the year.

Also for each month, we list a few practical ideas for becoming the answer to our prayers. Too often we use prayer as a substitute for action. But it seems that much of the time when we ask God to do something about pain and suffering, we hear God say back to us, "I already *did* do something — I made you." Our little lists are meant to provoke the imagination with ideas on how we might put our prayers into action and our faith into practice. They're meant as brainstorms to get the gears going, so feel free to add to those lists your own recipes for holy mischief.

Occasional Prayers

Partway through the book, you will find some prayers for special occasions. We have significantly shortened this section for the pocket edition, but we have added a few prayers we thought would be good for folks traveling or praying on their own.

Website

We could not fit in everything we wanted to include, even in the six-hundred pager, so we hope you'll check out the website and add your ideas to the mix: *www.commonprayer.net*. This may also be a helpful tool if you don't have the book handy or want to make copies of something or need to find a song or two. You can also connect with others who are praying *Common Prayer* together on Facebook.

Acknowledgments

Sometimes it has felt like this book took centuries to create —
and really it has.

There are lots of fingerprints on this book. Some of them are
ancient, and there are far too many people to name. But there are
some more contemporary collaborators we do want to recognize.
We have had a brilliant advisory team that gave us wisdom
and counsel along the way. Thanks to Phyllis Tickle, Sr. Karen
Mohan, Richard Rohr, Eliacin Rosario-Cruz, and Andy Raine.
We are especially grateful to Phyllis for her tremendous work
on the four-volume manual of prayer *The Divine Hours*, from
which we benefited immensely. And we are grateful to Andy and
the Northumbria Community for creating *Celtic Daily Prayer*,
and for their enthusiasm for our project. Both Phyllis and Andy
allowed us to raid and pillage their wisdom and work.

As we sensed the Spirit's motion in creating this book, we
gathered a dozen or so folks in North Carolina from different
traditions, many of them liturgy and prayer experts (if there is
such a thing). We put our hands together and said, "Let's do it."
That set things in motion. Thanks to Scott Bass and Roberta
Mothershead, who hosted that original gathering at Nazareth
House, and Catherine and Pete Askew, Karen Sloan, Monica
Klepac, Melanie Baffes, Katie Piche, Richard and Diana Twiss,
Christine Sine, Scott Krueger, Mark Van Steenwyck, Chris Haw,
Martin Shannon, and the many others who contributed the songs
and prayers that are written on their walls and in their hearts.
Their fingerprints are on this book.

Joel Klepac, Jesce Walz, and Rick Beerhorst were our fantastic
woodcut artists. Katie Jo Claiborne and Brian Gorman poured
in countless hours along the way editing, notating, praying, and
researching. We are grateful for our tremendous friends Angela

Scheff, Brian Phipps, and all the folks at Zondervan who have plotted with us and published this book.

And we have been your compilers. It has been an honor.

Now, add your fingerprints.

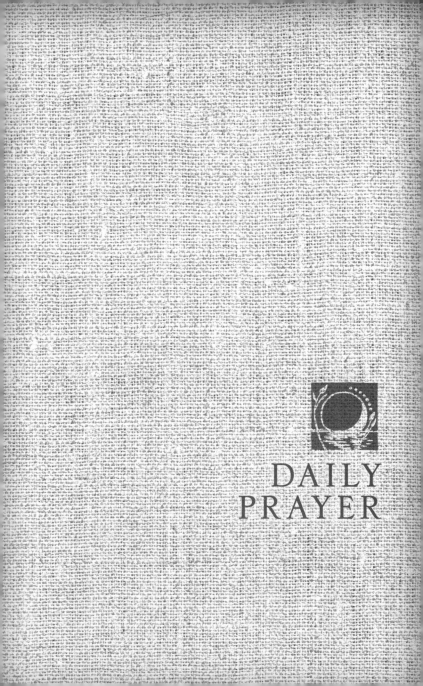

DAILY
PRAYER

✸ Morning Prayer

O Lord, let my soul rise up to meet you
as the day rises to meet the sun.

**Glory to the Father, and to the Son, and to the Holy
    Spirit,**
**as it was in the beginning, is now, and will be forever.
    Amen.**

Come, let us bow down and bend the knee : let us kneel before
    the LORD our Maker.

Song

In our lives and in our prayers : may your kingdom come.

Psalm

In our lives and in our prayers : may your kingdom come.

Scripture

In our lives and in our prayers : may your kingdom come.

Prayers for Others

Our Father

Lord God, almighty and everlasting Father, you have brought us
in safety to this new day. Preserve us now by your mighty power
that we may not fall into sin nor be overcome by adversity, and
in all that we do direct us to the fulfillment of your purposes,
through Jesus Christ our Lord. Amen.

May the peace of the Lord Christ go with you : wherever he may send you;

may he guide you through the wilderness : protect you through the storm;

may he bring you home rejoicing : at the wonders he has shown you;

may he bring you home rejoicing : once again into our doors.

 Midday Prayer

Draw us into your love, Christ Jesus : **and deliver us from fear.**

Lord, make me an instrument of your peace.
Where there is hatred, let me bring love;
where there is injury, pardon;
where there is doubt, faith;
where there is despair, hope;
where there is darkness, light;
where there is sadness, joy.
O Divine Master, grant that I may not
so much seek to be consoled as to console,
to be understood as to understand,
to be loved as to love.
For it is in giving that we receive,
it is in pardoning that we are pardoned,
and it is in dying that we are born to eternal life.

Glory to the Father, and to the Son, and to the Holy
    Spirit,
as it was in the beginning, is now, and will be forever.
    Amen.

Silence for meditation

Our Father

Make us worthy, Lord, to serve our brothers and sisters
throughout the world, who live and die in poverty and pain. Give
them today, through our hands, their daily bread; and through
our understanding love, give peace and joy. Amen.

Blessed are the poor,
for theirs is the kingdom of God.
Blessed are the hungry,

for they shall be filled.
Blessed are the meek,
for they shall inherit the earth.
Blessed are the pure in heart,
for they shall see God.
Blessed are those who mourn,
for they shall be comforted.
Blessed are the merciful,
for they shall be shown mercy.
Blessed are the peacemakers,
for they are the children of God.
Blessed are those who are persecuted for righteousness and
    justice,
for great is their reward.

Come, Holy Spirit. We pray that your fruit would be in us : love,
joy, peace, patience, kindness, goodness, faithfulness, gentleness,
and self-control.

Dear Jesus, help us to spread your fragrance everywhere we go.

Soul of Christ, sanctify me;
body of Christ, save me;
blood of Christ, inebriate me;
water from the side of Christ, wash me;
passion of Christ, strengthen me.
O good Jesus, hear me;
within your wounds hide me;
suffer me not to be separated from you;
from the malicious enemy defend me;
in the hour of my death call me;
and bid me come to you
that with your saints I may praise you
forever and ever. Amen.

Through our lives and by our prayers : may your kingdom come!

In the name of the Father, and of the Son, and of the Holy Spirit. Amen.

Passing the Peace

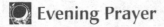 # Evening Prayer

Naked I came from my mother's womb, and naked will I return.
**The Lord gives, and the Lord takes away. Blessed be the
name of the Lord.**

O God, come to my assistance : **O Lord, make haste to help
me.**

**Glory to the Father, and to the Son, and to the Holy
Spirit,
as it was in the beginning, is now, and will be forever.
Amen.**

Kneeling **Lord, have mercy. Christ, have mercy. Lord, have
mercy.**

**I confess to almighty God,
and to you, my brothers and sisters,
that I have sinned through my own fault,
in my thoughts and in my words,
in what I have done,
and in what I have failed to do;
and I ask you, my brothers and sisters,
to pray for me to the Lord our God.**

Silence (or time to confess to God or to one another)

Rebuke me, O Lord, but not in your anger, lest I come to nothing.

Rising **Lord, have mercy. Christ, have mercy. Lord, have
mercy. Amen.**

A candle is lit during the following song
**Walk in the light, the beautiful light.
Come where the dewdrops of mercy shine bright.**

Shine all around us by day and by night.
Jesus, the light of the world.

O gracious Light,
pure brightness of the ever-living Father in heaven,
O Jesus Christ, holy and blessed!

Now as we come to the setting of the sun,
and our eyes behold the evening light,
we sing your praises, O God: Father, Son, and Holy Spirit.

You are worthy at all times to be praised by happy voices,
O Son of God, O Giver of life,
your glory fills the whole world.

In word or song
Praise God from whom all blessings flow.
Praise God all creatures here below.
Praise God above, ye heavenly host.
Praise Father, Son, and Holy Ghost. Amen.

Declaration of Faith
We believe and trust in God the Father Almighty.
We believe and trust in Jesus Christ, his Son.
We believe and trust in the Holy Spirit.
We believe and trust in the Three in One.

Prayers for Others
(following each request): **Lord, hear our prayer.**

Our Father

Magnificat (Mary's Song)
My soul glorifies the Lord,
my spirit rejoices in God my Savior.

**The Lord looks on me, a lowly servant; henceforth all
   ages will call me blessed.
The Almighty works marvels for me. Holy is God's name!
God's mercy is from age to age, on those who are faithful.
God puts forth an arm in strength and scatters the proud-
   hearted —
casts the mighty from their thrones and raises the lowly.
God fills the hungry with good things and sends the rich
   away empty,
protecting Israel, God's servant, remembering mercy,
the mercy promised to our ancestors,
to Abraham, Sarah, and their children forever.**

Visit this place, O Lord, and drive far from it all snares of the
enemy. Send your holy angels to dwell with us and preserve us
in peace. And let your blessing be upon us always, through Jesus
Christ our Lord. Amen.

**May the Lord bless us and keep us from all harm, and
   may God lead us to eternal life. Amen.**

✠ Compline

Search me, O God, and know my heart : test me and know my
thoughts.
See if there is any wicked way in me : and lead me in your way of
life.

Glory to the Father, and to the Son, and to the Holy Spirit,
as it was in the beginning, is now, and will be forever. Amen.

*A time of silence is kept to review the day, celebrating signs of
God's reign in the world, confessing sins, and lamenting the
systems of death that still hold power in our world.*

Holy, holy, holy, Lord,
God of power and might,
heaven and earth are full of your glory.
Hosanna in the highest.
Blessed is he who comes in the name of the Lord.
Hosanna in the highest.

I will lie down and sleep in peace; for you alone, Lord, make me
dwell in safety.

Psalm 134
Behold now, bless the LORD, all you servants of the LORD : you
that stand by night in the house of the LORD.
Lift up your hands in the holy place and bless the LORD : the
LORD who made heaven and earth bless you out of Zion.

I will lie down and sleep in peace; for you alone, Lord, make me
dwell in safety.

This is what we are about: we plant the seeds that will one day
grow. We water seeds already planted, knowing that they hold
promise. We lay foundations that will need further development.

We provide yeast that produces effects far beyond our capabilities.

We cannot do everything, and there is a sense of liberation in realizing that. This enables us to do something, and to do it well. It may be incomplete, but it is a beginning, a step along the way, an opportunity for the Lord's grace to enter and do the rest.

We may never see the results, but that is the difference between the master builder and the worker. We are workers, not master builders; ministers, not messiahs. We are prophets of a future not our own.

I will lie down and sleep in peace, for you alone, Lord, make me dwell in safety.

Into your hands, O Lord, I commend my spirit. For you have redeemed me, O Lord, O God of truth. Keep me, O Lord, as the apple of your eye; hide me under the shadow of your wings.

Keep watch, dear Lord, with those who work or watch or weep this night, and give your angels charge over those who sleep. Tend the sick, Lord Christ, give rest to the weary, bless the dying, soothe the suffering, pity the afflicted, shield the joyous, and all for your love's sake. Amen.

MONTHLY
ACTION

Marks of New Monasticism

Locating Our Lives in the Abandoned Places of the Empire

Everything in our society teaches us to move away from suffering, to move out of neighborhoods where there is high crime, to move away from people who don't look like us. But the gospel calls us to something altogether different. We are to laugh at fear, to lean into suffering, to open ourselves to the stranger. Advent is the season when we remember that Jesus put on flesh and moved into the neighborhood.

God's getting born in a barn reminds us that God shows up even in the forsaken corners of the earth.

NATIVITY

Movements throughout church history have gone to the desert, to the slums, to the most difficult places on earth to follow Jesus. For some of us, that means remaining in difficult neighborhoods that we were born into, even though folks may think we are crazy for not moving out. For others, it means returning to a difficult neighborhood after heading off to college or job training to acquire skills, choosing to bring those skills back to where we came from to help restore the broken streets. And for others, it may mean relocating our lives from places of so-called privilege to abandoned places to offer our gifts for God's kingdom.

Wherever we come from, Jesus teaches us that good can happen where we are, even if real-estate agents and politicians aren't interested in our neighborhoods. Jesus comes from Nazareth, a town from which folks said nothing good could come. He knew suffering from the moment he entered the world as a baby refugee born into a genocide. Jesus knew poverty and pain until he was tortured and executed on a Roman cross. This is the Jesus we are called to follow. With his coming, we learn that the most dangerous place for Christians to be is in comfort and safety, detached from the suffering of others. Places that are physically safe can be spiritually deadly.

One of the best stories of community in the United States comes from the backwoods of Georgia. In the 1940s, long before the civil rights movement had begun to question the racial divisions in the South, white folks and black folks came together to start Koinonia Farm — a "demonstration plot" for the kingdom of God, as they called it. Koinonia survived attacks from the Ku Klux Klan in the '50s and '60s, tilling the soil and sowing seeds for God's movement in the least likely of places.

Suggested Reading for the Month

Sayings of the Desert Mothers and Fathers

Jesus and the Disinherited by Howard Thurman

The Beloved Community by Charles Marsh

Becoming the Answer to Our Prayers: A Few Ideas

1. Throw a banquet, a really good one with lots of nice food. Invite folks who struggle with homelessness, mental illness, or addiction. Give everyone a chance to share a gift.

2. Do a creative witness outside a shopping mall. And be nice. Invite folks to see that the best things in life are free. Maybe give out coffee or cookies.

3. Dismantle a bomb. Or dismantle a theological argument that justifies bombs. Or dismantle an ideology of security and consumption that requires bombs.

4. Experiment in creation care by going fuel-free for a week —
   bike, carpool, or walk.

5. Start a business whose goal is to provide living-wage jobs to
   persons from economically disinvested neighborhoods.

Marks of New Monasticism

Shared Economics

Throughout Scripture, we are given a vision of an economy different from the empire's economy. One of the first stories in Scripture is of God's rescuing the Hebrew slaves from Egypt. God gives them new patterns of Sabbath as well as the practice of gleaning to make sure that they care for the most vulnerable among them (widows, orphans, immigrants). God also sets

THE BAPTISM OF CHRIST

in place Jubilee — God's systemic plan for dismantling inequality, relinquishing debts, redistributing property, setting slaves free, and allowing the land to rest and restore itself. There is the promise throughout Scripture that God has created an economy in which there is enough, that God has not created a world of scarcity with too many people and too little stuff. As Gandhi said, "There is enough for everyone's need, but not enough for everyone's greed."

We are to pray this day for our daily bread — nothing more and nothing less. Prophets such as John the Baptist call us to repentance but then also say things like, "And if you have two tunics, give one away to the person who has none." Rebirth and redistribution must go together. Just as Jesus came preaching repentance, he also invited his followers to sell everything they had and give the money to the poor. The early Christians went so far as to say that if we have two coats, we have stolen one from the poor, and that when we give to a beggar, we should get down on our knees and ask for forgiveness, because we are returning what was stolen from that person.

Economic sharing was a mark of the early church. Scripture says, "No one claimed that any of their possessions was their own, but they shared everything they had.... There were no needy persons among them" (Acts 4:32, 34). One of the signs of the birth of the church is that the first Christians ended poverty among themselves. But it was not just a systemic thing; it was a love thing. The Scriptures say that we can sell everything we have and give the money to the poor, but if we have not love, our actions are empty. For Christians, redistribution comes out of a love of neighbor; to love our neighbor as ourselves means we hold our possessions loosely, for the suffering of another is our suffering, and another's burden is our burden.

Creative experiments in economic sharing are being carried out all over the world. One group of Christians in the United States started putting out a newsletter listing everyone in the group who was hospitalized and unable to cover their medical bills, so that everyone could pray for each other and then put their money together to pay the bills. Over the past few decades, that group has paid more than five hundred million dollars in medical bills. Another fascinating experiment is the Relational Tithe, an international group of Christians who tithe (give 10 percent of their income) into a common fund to meet one another's needs and the needs of people they are friends with. That one hundred percent of their tithe goes directly to meet needs is the witness of a community that bears each other's burdens. Rebirth comes with responsibility, for we are reborn into a dysfunctional family. And redistribution, most meaningfully, comes not through guilt or coercion but through compassion, solidarity, and love.

Suggested Reading for the Month

Sabbath Economics by Ched Myers

Rich Christians in an Age of Hunger by Ron Sider

God's Economy by Jonathan Wilson-Hartgrove

Economy of Love by Relational Tithe

Becoming the Answer to Our Prayers: A Few Ideas

1. Try to go a whole week without spending any money. If you have to, barter or beg a little to make it through.

2. Hold a Baby Goods Exchange for parents to bring toys and clothing their kids have outgrown and trade them.

3. Join a Bible study led by someone who has less formal education than yourself.

4. Attempt to repair something that is broken. Appreciate the people who repair things for you on a regular basis.

5. Defy complacency and flout despair. Believe that you can do something, right now, right here — even if you take only a baby step.

FEBRUARY

Marks of New Monasticism

Reconciliation

We lament racial division within the church and pursue a just reconciliation. Martin Luther King Jr. powerfully called out one of the most heartbreaking ironies for those of us who call ourselves Christians: "The most segregated hour in the world is eleven o'clock on Sunday morning" — when we gather for worship. Of all the places we should hope and expect to see the diversity of God's family, it is not in the shopping malls and bars but in the church. But reconciliation begins on a small scale. It must begin in living rooms and at dinner tables. Reconciliation will never make its way into our worship services until it makes its way into our homes.

THE PUBLICAN
AND THE PHARISEE

During Black History Month, we acknowledge the many ways racism has crippled our country, while also celebrating African-Americans who've made incredible contributions to society. Alongside the ugly stories in the bloodstained pages of church history, in which Christians justified slavery and genocide with deadly theology, there are the incredible stories of communities of faith who lived with great courage in times of oppression and conflict. In South Africa, a community of black and white South Africans bought land together and began living on it in the middle of apartheid. Their lives were at risk. They were threatened with jail time. Their kingdom-minded friendships were an offense to their society of colonialism and segregation. Reconciliation takes different shapes in different contexts and eras. There are beautiful stories of Catholics and Protestants in Northern Ireland, and Hutus and Tutsis in Burundi, starting communities where they live and worship together, lamenting their history of Christians killing other Christians. These communities are a prophetic witness and a healing leaven amid a world still riddled with racism and prejudice and hatred.

When we make reconciliation our goal, we don't pretend to have it all together. Like the tax collector who beat his chest in the back of the temple, saying, "Lord, have mercy," we begin our prayer for reconciliation with lament and repentance. With us, reconciliation is impossible. But with God, all things are possible. We don't just believe it; we've seen it.

Suggested Reading for the Month

Let Justice Roll Down by John Perkins

No Future without Forgiveness by Desmond Tutu

Mirror to the Church by Emmanuel Katongole

Grace Matters by Chris Rice

Becoming the Answer to Our Prayers: A Few Ideas

1. Mow your neighbor's grass.

2. Create a directory of spiritual mentors and help folks find them.

3. Practice radical hospitality, which includes the willingness to be a guest. Next time you make a vacation or business trip, stay in homes instead of hotels.

4. Ask the next person who asks you for change to join you for dinner.

5. Invest money in a micro-lending bank.

Marks of New Monasticism

Celebrating Singleness and Marriage

Both singleness and marriage are gifts to the church. Both can teach us about God. Both can be holy, and both can be self-centered. There are lots of books on marriage, and still the Christian divorce rate mirrors that of the larger society. We have much work to do, and there aren't many good books out there on singleness or celibacy, a traditional monastic vow.

THE ANNUNCIATION

Singleness is often terribly misunderstood. Catholics have often overemphasized singleness and the religious vocation of celibacy to the point that folks feel defeated if they don't end up being a nun, a priest, or a monk. (It is said that John Newton was asked if he was a monk, and he replied, "God hasn't given me the grace ... so I am only a monk on Mondays and Wednesdays.") And Protestants have nearly forgotten the gift that singleness is. Many singles groups end up being little more than an opportunity to meet a spouse. Pastors pray that every kid will find the mate that God has chosen for them, forgetting the gift of singleness that Paul spoke so highly of and that Jesus celebrates when he holds up those who have "renounced marriage because of the kingdom of heaven" (Matt. 19:12). We cannot forget the saints throughout church history whose singleness has been part of their radical faith and single-minded pursuit of God as their Lover and Soul Mate. After all, when we think of Mother Teresa, we don't say

47

pityingly, "If only she had met her husband!" A life of singleness helped free her up for a single-minded pursuit of God's kingdom.

March is Women's History Month. It's also when the church remembers Mary, the first of the saints, a woman who put her sexuality in the service of God's kingdom, giving birth to our Lord and thereby becoming mother to all of us. With Mary as our mother and Jesus as our brother, we are part of God's family whether we marry or remain single. Whatever the case, we know love because we've been adopted into God's family.

Our deepest longing is not for sex but for love. We can live without sex, but we cannot live without love. And there certainly are many folks who have a lot of sex but never find love, and others who may never have sex but who have found love and intimacy in the deepest core of their being. We are created to love and be loved. Marriage and biological family is a beautiful place to find love. But it is not the only place, and that is good news to the singles out there and to the many folks who do not find themselves attracted to the opposite sex. If our communities can create spaces where people can love and be loved as God has loved us, all the other stuff gets a little bit easier.

Suggested Reading for the Month

The Wounded Healer by Henri Nouwen

Real Sex by Lauren Winner

Families at the Crossroads by Rodney Clapp

The Life of Amma Syncletica or *The Life of St. Macrina*

Becoming the Answer to Our Prayers: A Few Ideas

1. Take a break from noise. For a day or a week, turn off things that make noise, and spend the time in silence, speaking only when necessary. Also remember those in our world whose voices have been silenced.

2. Go to a home for the elderly and ask for a list of folks who don't get any visitors. Visit them each week and tell stories, read together, or play board games.

3. Laugh at advertisements, especially ones that teach you that you can buy happiness.

4. Go down a line of parked cars and add money to the meters that are expired. Leave a little note saying something nice.

5. Connect with a group of migrant workers or farmers who grow your food. Visit their farm. Maybe even pick some veggies with them. Ask what they get paid.

APRIL

Marks of New Monasticism

Submission to Christ's Body, the Church

Discontentment is a gift to the church. If you have the ability to see the things that are wrong in the church and in the world, you should thank God for that perception. Not everyone has the eyes to notice or to care. But we must also see that our discontentment is not a reason to disengage from the church but a reason to engage with it. As Gandhi said, "Be the change you want to see in the world." Our invitation is to "be the change" we want to see in the church. There are things worth protesting, but we also have to be people who "pro-testify," proclaiming the kingdom that we're for, not just the evils we're against.

Jesus offered an alternative to Caesar's empire not by mounting a rebellion but by teaching people that another way is possible. That way is illustrated well by Jesus' triumphal entry, the inaugural parade of a new kind of king for a new kind of kingdom. Church history is filled with holy dissenters, rabble-rousers, and prophets — disturbers of the peace who've helped to show us a better way. As some church historians have pointed out, every few hundred years the church gets cluttered by the materialism and militarism of the world around it. We begin to forget who we are. One bishop said, "And so every five hundred years or so the church needs a rummage sale," to get rid of the clutter and to remember the true treasures of our faith.

Church history is filled with reformations and renewals. It was in the middle of Italy's prosperity and crusades that St. Francis heard God whisper, "Repair my church, which is in ruins," and

he began to repair the ruins. At one point, the pope had a vision that the church was beginning to crumble, but the corner was being held up by Francis and the little youth movement in Assisi. The call to repair the church is a call we continue to hear from God, and a movement we are invited to participate in.

THE TRIUMPHAL ENTRY

We shouldn't be too surprised that the church is a mess. After all, it's made up of people. Augustine said, "The church is a whore, but she's our mother." The early Christians said that if we do not accept the church as our mother, we cannot call God our Father. We are not to leave her, but we are to work for her healing, as we would for a dysfunctional parent's healing. Our work is not "para-church" but "pro-church." The church needs our discontent, and we need the rest of the body of Christ. One pastor said it like this: "The church is sort of like Noah's ark. It's a stinky mess inside, but if you get out, you'll drown."

Suggested Reading for the Month

The Great Emergence by Phyllis Tickle

Beyond Smells and Bells by Mark Galli

For the Life of the World by Alexander Schmemann

Becoming the Answer to Our Prayers: A Few Ideas

1. Track to its source one item of food you eat regularly. Then each time you eat that food, remember the folks who made it possible for you to consume it.

2. Become a pen pal with someone who is in prison.

3. Try recycling water from the washer or sink by using it to flush your toilet. Remember the 1.2 billion folks who don't have clean water.

4. Leave a tip for someone cleaning the streets or the public restroom.

5. Write one CEO each month this year. Affirm or critique the ethics of their companies. (You may need to do a little research first.)

MAY

Marks of New Monasticism

Hospitality

Hospitality is one of the marks of the early church. Jesus was always going to people's homes, and his healings and teaching often happened around a dinner table or in a living room. The early church met and ate in each other's homes. It has been noted that when the disciples were sent out with nothing at all (no money, no extra clothes, no provisions), it was not because Jesus wanted them to suffer in poverty or to be left alone in the street; it was because he wanted them to rely on the hospitality of others. Not only were the early Christians to practice hospitality; they were to depend on it. There was no "us" and "them." *My* became a cussword for Christians. My house is no longer mine but is God's, which means it is open to all.

One of the early Christians pointed out the miracle of hospitality and the abundance that comes from sharing, and said, "We have no house, but we have homes everywhere we go." Our Mennonite brothers and sisters have known this for a long time; they created

CHRIST

a directory of Christian homes that are open to folks who are in crisis or who are traveling and need a place to stay (before there was couchhopper.com!). Dorothy Day and the Catholic Worker Movement also shared this vision of hospitality and insisted that if every Christian home made room for the stranger, we would end poverty and homelessness.

Our Savior came into the world dependent on hospitality, from the moment he was born in a borrowed manger until he was buried in a donated tomb. What is more, Jesus longs to meet us face to face in the disguise of the stranger, of the guest at our door. Christ looks at us longingly, as in our icon for this month, eager for us to answer the call and invite him into our lives.

There are beautiful stories of Christian hospitality from all over the world. One of our favorites comes from Christians living along the border of the United States and Mexico. They, like many of us, became deeply concerned about the struggles of undocumented brothers and sisters and the plight of many recent immigrants to the US. They insisted that laws don't dictate how we are to treat immigrants, but Scripture does, and unquestionably the Bible speaks about a God of hospitality and grace, who is a refuge to the widow and orphan and alien. As God's people, we are to be like that. So these Christians on the border opened up their homes as sanctuary houses and helped undocumented friends get legal help. But they did not stop there. They decided they also wanted their lives to be a witness to the world, so they organized worship services along the border, in which hundreds of Christians on the Mexican side of the wall joined hundreds of Christians on the US side. There they worshiped Jesus together. And then they served each other communion by throwing it over the wall.

Suggested Reading for the Month

Making Room by Christine Pohl
Selected Writings of Dorothy Day

Becoming the Answer to Our Prayers: A Few Ideas

1. Wash your clothes by hand and dry them on a line. Remember the 1.6 billion people who do not have electricity.

2. Learn to sew. Try making your own clothes for a year.

3. Eat only one bowl of rice a day for a week. (Be sure also to take a multivitamin.) And remember the twenty-five thousand people who die of malnutrition and starvation each day.

4. Keep the Sabbath holy. Rest one day a week this year — don't answer the phone or the door, and don't use the internet. Do something that brings you life that day.

5. Go to a city council meeting. Pray. Speak as the Spirit leads.

Marks of New Monasticism

Care for Creation

Fifty days after Pentecost Sunday, the church celebrates the Holy Trinity, worshiping the one God who lives and reigns forever as Father, Son, and Holy Spirit. The Holy Trinity icon is a reminder that Abraham and Sarah welcomed God in three visitors who showed up at their door. Theology is never far removed from the people and places outside our doors.

Sometimes our theology is so concentrated on heaven that it invalidates any concern for the earth. Some images in Scripture have even been misconstrued to perpetuate a disregard for creation, such as the image that in the last days the world will be consumed by fire. But nearly every other time the "consumed by fire" image is evoked in Scripture, it is a fire that purifies rather than burns up, a fire that frees up life rather than destroys it. No doubt, the way we live is shaped by how we imagine the end of the world — whether we think God's final plan is for everything to go up in flames or for everything to be brought back to life.

THE HOLY TRINITY

Creation care is not just about theology. It is about having the creativity to embody our theology imaginatively — flushing toilets with dirty sink water, riding a bike to work as an act of prophetic dissent, or helping an institution become carbon neutral. At its core, creation care is about loving our global neighbor, because the poor suffer the most from the degradation of the earth and the struggle for clean water. Many kids in the concrete jungle of the ghettoes and slums are so disconnected from creation that they feel disconnected from the Creator.

A community of folks moved into Camden, New Jersey, because the neighborhood has suffered so deeply from environmental degradation that it was rated one of the worst places to live in America. More than half the kids have chronic asthma. But part of what we do as we plant urban gardens is to reconnect to the beauty of the earth. Kids get to see grass pierce concrete. Their eyes light up as they pull a carrot out of the ground, and digging for potatoes can feel like digging up lost treasure. At the heart of it all is a God who so loved the world and who called everything in it good. Our story began in a garden, but it ends in a city — a beautiful restored city the Scriptures describe as the New Jerusalem, coming on earth as it is in heaven. Christianity is not just about going up to heaven when we die; it's about bringing God's kingdom down, all the way to the dirt in our gardens.

Suggested Reading for the Month

For the Beauty of the Earth by Stephen Bouma-Prediger

Serve God, Save the Planet by Matthew Sleeth

Go Green, Save Green by Nancy Sleeth

Eaarth by Bill McKibben

Becoming the Answer to Our Prayers: A Few Ideas

1. Hang out with folks who will inherit the earth. (For details, see the Sermon on the Mount.)

2. Set up a retreat center with pastoral care and spiritual guidance — free of charge — for persons who have little money.

3. Look through your clothes. Learn about one of the countries where they are manufactured. Do some research to discover the working conditions of the people who made them, and

commit to doing one thing to improve the lives of people who live in that country.

4. Look for everything you have two of, and give one away.

5. Dig up a bucket of soil and look through it to see the elements and organisms that make our daily meals possible.

Marks of New Monasticism

Geographical Proximity

There is something to be said for a "theology of place" — choosing to orient our lives around community for the sake of the gospel. In many of the wealthiest countries in the world, we have lost the sense of a village. So much of our culture is oriented around moving away from people rather than closer to them. We live in a mobile culture in which people are used to moving every few years, and in which many folks will uproot

JOACHIM AND ANNA

without question to move for a higher-paying job. We have some of the highest rates of home ownership and some of the highest rates of depression. We are some of the wealthiest *and* loneliest societies the world has ever seen.

Commitment to a people and a place is one of the countercultural values at the heart of the gospel. It recaptures the notion of the parish, a word which shares a root with *parochial*, meaning "localized and particular." Many folks these days are learning from village cultures, in which people often have fewer resources but more life and joy. Even our geography has to be rethought, because our neighborhoods and homes are often built around values different from the gospel and community. What we often lament as a "breakdown of the family" is really a breakdown of local community, which has stripped away the support structures that help all of us survive. Joachim and Anna, whom tradition names as Jesus' maternal grandparents and who nurtured the mother of the Lord, remind us how important the basic institutions of family and community are.

Movements of co-housing and new urbanism are helping to cultivate spaces for shared life. People in one cul-de-sac began to rethink suburban sprawl and started sharing stuff. They decided each home didn't need a washer and dryer and a lawn mower. So one family agreed to have the laundry machines, and another had all the lawn equipment, and so on. Before long, they were homeschooling their kids together and providing hospitality to the homeless with all of the energy and resources they freed up by sharing. When people make choices like these, life starts to look like a village, and a village is a beautiful thing.

Suggested Reading for the Month

Sex, Economy, Freedom and Community by Wendell Berry

Theology as Big as the City by Ray Bakke

The Wisdom of Stability by Jonathan Wilson-Hartgrove

Becoming the Answer to Our Prayers: A Few Ideas

1. Begin a scholarship fund so that for every one of your own children you send to college, you can create a scholarship for an at-risk youth. Get to know these youths' families and learn from each other.

2. Visit a worship service in which you will be a minority. Invite someone to a meal after the service.

3. Confess something you have done wrong to someone whom you have wronged or offended, and ask for forgiveness.

4. Serve in a homeless shelter. For extra credit, go back to that shelter and eat or sleep there and allow yourself to be served.

5. Go through a local thrift store and drop dollar bills in the pockets of clothing in the store.

AUGUST

Marks of New Monasticism

Peacemaking

Peace is not just the absence of conflict; it's also the presence of justice. Martin Luther King Jr. even distinguished between "the devil's peace" and God's true peace. A counterfeit peace exists when people are pacified or distracted or so beat up and tired of fighting that all seems calm. But true peace does not exist until there is justice, restoration, forgiveness.

Peacemaking doesn't mean passivity. It is the act of interrupting injustice without mirroring injustice, the act of disarming evil without destroying the evildoer, the act of finding a third way that is neither fight nor flight but the careful, arduous pursuit of reconciliation and justice. It is about a revolution of love that is big enough to set both the oppressed and the oppressors free. Peacemaking is about being able to recognize in the face of the oppressed our own faces, and in the hands of the oppressors our own hands.

Peacemaking, like most beautiful things, begins small. Matthew 18 gives us a clear process for making peace with someone who has hurt or offended us; first we are to talk directly with them, not at them or around them. Most communities that have been around a while (like a few decades or centuries) identify "straight talk," or creating an environment where people do not avoid conflict but speak honestly to one another, as one of the core values of healthy community. Straight talk is countercultural in a world that prefers politeness to honesty. In his *Rule*, Benedict of Nursia speaks passionately about the deadly poison of "murmuring," the negativity and dissension that can infect community and rot the fabric of love.

Peacemaking begins with what we can change — ourselves. But it doesn't end there. We are to be peacemakers in a world riddled with violence. That means interrupting violence with imagination, on our streets and in our world. Peacemaking "that is not like any way the empire brings peace" is rooted in the nonviolence of the cross, where we see a Savior who loves his enemies so much he died for them. Peacemaking is often not our instinct, which is why it must be cultivated and grown in us. Even Jesus' key disciple, Peter, picks up his sword when the soldiers approach Jesus. Jesus' response is brilliant: he scolds Peter, and then he heals the wounded persecutor, only to be dragged away and hung on a Roman cross. If ever there were a case for "just war" or justified violence to protect the innocent, Peter has it. Yet Jesus refutes his logic of the sword.

THE TRANSFIGURATION

The early Christians said, "When Jesus disarmed Peter, he disarmed every Christian." For hundreds of years, Christians were never seen carrying swords, and they followed the way of the Prince of Peace even unto death, loving their enemies and blessing those who cursed them. It doesn't sound like a good strategy for running an empire, but it is the narrow way that leads to life. Undoubtedly, it doesn't always seem to "work." As we look at history, and even as we read the Scriptures, we seem to find evidence that violence has worked at times and failed at times, just as nonviolence seems to have worked at times and failed at times. In the end, the question is, Which looks most like Jesus? For we are called not just to be successful but to be faithful to the way of the cross, even unto death. The way of the cross might not seem to work on Friday, but Sunday is coming. In the end, Love wins.

This can be hard to remember as we go about our lives. But the transfiguration reminds us how the disciples' eyes were opened to the reality of Jesus' power even before the resurrection. If we have eyes to see, the lightning that flashes east to west in the nonviolent coming of God can illuminate the world wherever we are. "If you are willing," one of the desert fathers said, "you can become all flame."

Suggested Reading for the Month

The Politics of Jesus by John Howard Yoder

Resident Aliens by Stanley Hauerwas and William Willimon

The Powers That Be by Walter Wink

The Violence of Love by Oscar Romero

"Riverside Speech" by Martin Luther King Jr. (audio; good for August 6, the anniversary of the bombing of Hiroshima)

Becoming the Answer to Our Prayers: A Few Ideas

1. Build a little chapel or prayer room in your home or in the woods and start using it.

2. Do something that doesn't fit the status quo.

3. Forgive a politician, pastor, parent, or friend who has wronged you.

4. Serve at a free clinic for persons who are uninsured.

5. Let your yes be yes and your no be no.

Marks of New Monasticism

Contemplative Prayer

Over and over, Scripture invites us to abide in God. To rest in God. To dwell in God. More than fifty times, Paul repeats the phrase "in Christ." Contemplative prayer is not just about activity and speaking but also about listening and resting in God.

THE SAN DAMIANO CROSS

Many of us have grown up thinking of prayer as a checklist of requests to God, like giving a grocery list to someone headed to the supermarket. As one kid said, "I'm heading off to pray; does anyone need anything?" Prayer is certainly about sharing our concerns and frustrations with God. God is personal enough to come down and wrestle in the dirt with Jacob or answer Abraham's pleading on behalf of Sodom and Gomorrah. Still, contemplative prayer goes deeper. A primary purpose of prayer is to impress on us the personality and character of Christ. We want to become like Jesus, so the life that we live is no longer ours but Christ living in us and through us.

Prayer is less about trying to get God to do something we want God to do and more about getting ourselves to do what God wants us to do and to become who God wants us to become. There are times when we speak, weep, groan, and shout at God. But there are also times when we simply sit in silence and are held by our Beloved. We remember the character of God, the fruit of the Spirit, and the incarnation of Jesus as he reveals to us what God is like with flesh on. And we pray that God's character will become our character. The monks have been known to say,

"If your speaking doesn't add something beautiful to the silence, don't speak." For many of us in the high-paced, cluttered world of materialism and noise, silence is a way we can free up the space to listen to God.

Silence gets interrupted pretty quickly. Whether it's a knock at the door, a cry from the nursery, or thoughts in our own heads, something almost always breaks the silence we long for in contemplative prayer. It is tempting to give up, to say that silence is not possible in our context or "I'm not cut out for this." But the wisdom of those who've gone before is helpful here. Teresa of Avila, who was distracted by her own thoughts in prayer, said she learned not to fight them but to let them come and go like waves in the sea, trusting that God was an anchor who could hold her through any storm.

Contemplation is about tending to the lines that anchor us in Christ. For Francis of Assisi, the San Damiano cross was one of those lines, serving as an icon to focus his prayer on Christ's love. It was after hours of prayer before this cross that he heard Jesus say, "Rebuild my church, which is in ruins." Then he got up to start the most radical renewal movement of the Middle Ages. Activism that matters to the kingdom is always rooted in prayer. If we want to join God in changing the world, the place to begin is on our knees before the cross.

Suggested Reading for the Month

Contemplation in a World of Action by Thomas Merton

Selected Works of Teresa of Avila

Resistance and Contemplation by James Douglass

Becoming the Answer to Our Prayers: A Few Ideas

1. Track down old teachers and mentors. Let them know the influence they have had on your life.

2. Hold a ritual of prayerfully cutting up credit cards.

3. Move to a place that makes you uncomfortable, or visit a place where you will be a minority.

4. Ask your pastor to remove the US flag from the altar, or to include the flags of the other 195 countries of the world.

5. Babysit for someone free of charge, especially someone who might really need a night off and can't afford a sitter.

Marks of New Monasticism

Formation in the Way of Christ

For many of us, the judgmental, arrogant, legalistic Christianity we knew growing up created a suspicion of discipline and order that can lead to a pretty sloppy spirituality. Reacting against the institution's sickness, we easily find ourselves with little to help us heal our wounds, create new disciplines, and carve out a space where goodness triumphs. People who are afraid of spiritual discipline will not produce very good disciples.

SAINT FRANCIS

Community is pretty hip these days. We all have within us a longing for community. We long to love and to be loved. But if community doesn't exist for something beyond ourselves, it will atrophy, suffocate, die. *Discipline* and *disciple* share the same root; without discipline, we become little more than hippie communes or frat houses. We easily fall short of God's dream to form a new humanity with distinct practices that offer hope and good news to the world. Every culture has distinct ways of eating and partying; the ways of those of us who follow Jesus are different from the culture of consumption, homogeniety, and hedonism. Our homes, our living rooms, even our parties can become places of solace and hospitality for those with addictions and struggles. But it doesn't happen accidentally. Dorothy Day said, "We have to create an environment where it is easier to be good."

St. Francis of Assisi is a model for us not only of what it looks like to follow hard after Jesus but also of how we can celebrate the disciplines that have been passed down to us and become the church that we long for, even among people who've given up on "church." Our communities should be places where people can detox, whether that be from alcohol, tobacco, gluttony, shopping, or gossip. We long for a space that tips us toward goodness rather than away from it, where we can pick up new habits — holy habits — as we are formed into a new creation, transformed by God.

Suggested Reading for the Month

Celebration of Discipline by Richard Foster

The Spiritual Exercises of St. Ignatius of Loyola

The Rule of St. Benedict

Becoming the Answer to Our Prayers: A Few Ideas

1. Start setting aside 10 percent of your income to give away to folks in need.

2. Write letters (by hand on paper) for a month. Try writing to someone who needs encouragement or to whom you should say, "I'm sorry."

3. Contact your local crisis pregnancy center and invite a pregnant woman to live with your family.

4. Go without food for one day to remember the two billion people who live on less than a dollar a day.

5. Find a piece of land and care for it. Create a little guerilla garden, and participate with God to help it bear food and flowers. Have kids help out or get a school or youth group involved.

NOVEMBER

Marks of New Monasticism

Nurturing a Common Life

Independence is a value of our culture, but it is not a gospel value. Jesus lived in community and was part of a village culture. Remember the incident in his youth when his parents lost track of him for several days during the Passover festival (Luke 2)? Don't you sort of wonder how you lose your kid, especially when you are raising the Messiah? They were part of a village, traveling together, and probably trusting that he was in the good hands of some friend or family member. Jesus' culture was more like the Bedouins than the burbs.

The Scriptures teach us to value interdependence and community more highly than independence, and tell us that we are to lose our lives if we want to find them. Forming our lives around something other than our desires, jobs, and goals is radically countercultural. Even our architecture is oriented around individual families, not around community. But for many Native Americans and tribal cultures, society and architecture are oriented around the idea of a village. Individual dwellings, like the tepee, are very small, and they are built around a central common space where people eat, dance, sing, and tell stories. The rampant individualism of Western society is a relatively new thing, and its emptiness is increasingly evident. We are wealthy and lonely. But God invites us into a common life with others. Rather than build our lives around the individualistic dream of a house with a white picket fence, we build our lives around God's vision for community.

We dream of a holy village in the middle of the urban desert, with a little cluster of row homes sprinkled about and a neighborhood where folks are committed to God and to each other. Some folks are indigenous to the neighborhood. Some are missional relocators. Some have gone off to school, trained as doctors, lawyers, social workers, or business folk, and then returned to the neighborhood to offer their gifts to the work of restoration. The houses are small, but that is all we need — a place to lay our heads — because most of our lives are lived on the streets, on the stoop, sweating in the practice of resurrection. Village life begins by greeting the day in morning prayer, and in the evenings we share a meal or grill out on the street. Maybe there is a village center where folks can cook healthy breakfasts for the kids as they head off to school. Perhaps in that center there are laundry machines that we can all share and a game library where kids can borrow a game for the afternoon. Maybe there's a tool library so folks can check out a saw or a drill for the day; maybe there's an exercise space for lifting weights or taking an aerobics class to keep our bodies healthy. It's a dream of a village that shares things, that makes sure possessions and privileges are available for all, a place on earth where there truly is a "common wealth."

DOROTHY DAY

Shaping a life together sometimes begins simply by creating a space for community. For many intentional communities, that means we work only part-time so that we free up time for things we don't get paid to do, like welcoming homeless folks for a meal, helping neighborhood kids with homework, planting gardens on abandoned lots, or praying together each day. Sometimes we have to remove some of the clutter that occupies our time and energy, like getting rid of the television. But then, as we say no to some things, we say yes to others — cooking meals, painting murals, playing games. And most people don't miss the old life much anyway. A reporter once told Mother Teresa, "I wouldn't do what you do for a million dollars." She responded, "Me neither." We live in community and among the suffering because it is what we are made for. Not only does it give life to others, but it gives us life as well.

Suggested Reading for the Month

Life Together by Dietrich Bonhoeffer

Why We Live in Community by Eberhard Arnold

Community and Growth by Jean Vanier

Becoming the Answer to Our Prayers: A Few Ideas

1. Spend the day baking cookies or bread. Give them to the person who delivers your mail or picks up your trash.

2. Host a rain barrel party and teach neighbors how to capture water to use in the garden or for doing laundry.

3. Spend a day hiking in the woods. Consider how God cares for the lilies and the sparrows — and you.

4. Gather some neighbors and plant a tree in your neighborhood together.

5. Hold a knowledge exchange, in which you gather friends or neighbors to share a skill or something they are learning.

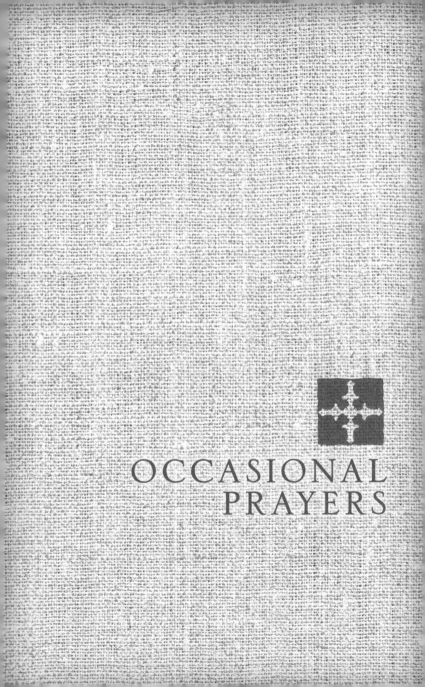

OCCASIONAL
PRAYERS

✝ An Affirmation of Faith

Lord, you have always given
bread for the coming day;
and though I am poor,
today I believe.

Lord, you have always given
strength for the coming day;
and though I am weak,
today I believe.

Lord, you have always given
peace for the coming day;
and though of anxious heart,
today I believe.

Lord, you have always kept me
safe in trials;
and now, tried as I am,
today I believe.

Lord, you have always marked
the road for the coming day;
and though it may be hidden,
today I believe.

Lord, you have always lightened
this darkness of mine;
and though the night is here,
today I believe.

Lord, you have always spoken
when time was ripe;
and though you be silent,
today I believe.

✣ A Franciscan Blessing

May God bless you with discomfort at easy answers, half-truths, and superficial relationships so that you may live deep within your heart.

May God bless you with anger at injustice, oppression, and exploitation of people, so that you may wish for justice, freedom, and peace.

May God bless you with enough foolishness to believe that you can make a difference in this world, so that you can do what others claim cannot be done.

✣ A Travel Blessing

May God, who is present in sunrise and nightfall
and in the crossing of the sea,
guide your feet as you go.

May God, who is with you when you sit
and when you stand,
encompass you with love
and lead you by the hand.

May God, who knows your path
and the places where you rest,
be with you in your waiting,
be your good news for sharing,
and lead you in the way that is everlasting.

✦ Prayers for Travelers and Pilgrims

Prayer of St. Patrick

Christ with me, Christ before me, Christ behind me,
Christ in me, Christ beneath me, Christ above me,
Christ on my right, Christ on my left,
Christ when I lie down, Christ when I sit down, Christ when I
    arise,
Christ in the heart of every man who thinks of me,
Christ in the mouth of everyone who speaks of me,
Christ in every eye that sees me,
Christ in every ear that hears me.

*St. Francis' Prayer**

Lord, make me an instrument of your peace.
Where there is hatred, let me sow love.
Where there is injury, pardon.
Where there is doubt, faith.
Where there is despair, hope.
Where there is darkness, light.
Where there is sadness, joy.
O Divine Master,
grant that I may not so much seek to be consoled as to console,
to be understood as to understand,
to be loved as to love.
For it is in giving that we receive,
it is in pardoning that we are pardoned,
and it is in dying that we are born to eternal life.
Amen.

✦ The Jesus Prayer

Lord Jesus Christ, Son of God, have mercy on me, a sinner.†

---

*This prayer is often attributed to St. Francis, though the source has not been accurately tracked
farther back than 1912. Nonetheless, we like it and use it often.

†This prayer is one of the most famous ancient prayers in the Eastern Orthodox tradition. It is

✠ For Deliverance from False Desires and Fears

Deliver me, O Jesus,
from the desire to be esteemed,
from the desire to be loved,
from the desire to be honored,
from the desire to be praised,
from the desire to be preferred to others,
from the desire to be consulted,
from the desire to be approved,
and from the desire to be popular.

Deliver me, O Jesus,
from the fear of being humiliated,
from the fear of being despised,
from the fear of being rebuked,
from the fear of being slandered,
from the fear of being forgotten,
from the fear of being wronged,
from the fear of being treated unfairly,
and from the fear of being suspected.

And, dear Jesus, grant me the grace
to desire that others might be more loved than I,
that others might be more esteemed than I,
that in the opinion of the world, others may increase
    and I decrease,
that others may be chosen and I may be set aside,
that others may be preferred to me in everything,
that others may become holier than I, provided that I, too,
    become as holy as I can.

---

a short prayer, often repeated over and over, and has been used by monks and pilgrims since at least the fifth century.

✠ Prayers against Bad Thoughts

Against Gluttony

Once again, Lord Jesus Christ, I face the power of gluttony.

Against the torrent of oblivion, I plead the blood of Jesus.

When my stomach aches and my mouth waters, teach me to hunger and thirst for justice.

When my body is tired and my spirit weak, give me grace to hide in your wounded side.

When I am tempted to turn from the way of the cross, help me to see the prize set before me.

Deliver me from gluttony, that whether I am fasting or feasting, my body's desire might be for your table, where none go hungry but all find bread that satisfies.

Lord Jesus Christ, Son of God, have mercy on me, a sinner.

Against Lust

Once again, Lord Jesus Christ, I face the power of lust.

Against the torrent of oblivion, I plead the blood of Jesus.

When my eyes are drawn to images that only stir up desire, turn them to the cross on which you died.

When my body longs for another to which it does not belong, draw me to your side as a dearly beloved bride.

When my thoughts turn toward pleasures which are not mine to enjoy, help me to imagine the pain of infidelity and the cost of broken trust.

Deliver me from lust, that I might embrace each soul and body as a sister or brother in you.

Lord Jesus Christ, Son of God, have mercy on me, a sinner.

Against the Love of Money

Once again, Lord Jesus Christ, I face the power of avarice.

Against the torrent of oblivion, I plead the blood of Jesus.

When I worry about survival and grasp for false security, remind me of the boy who shared his meal so you could feed the multitudes.

When I am tempted to store up treasure in savings accounts, help me to make eternal investments in your kingdom and trust your economy of love.

When I wonder who will care for me when I am old, give me elders to love and young friends to mentor in your way of abundant life.

Deliver me from avarice, that I might know the love that casts out fear and receive the gift of your provision through another's hand.

Lord Jesus Christ, Son of God, have mercy on me, a sinner.

Against Sadness

Once again, Lord Jesus Christ, I face the power of sadness.

Against the torrent of oblivion, I plead the blood of Jesus.

When I do not get what I want, even when I think it is what you want, give me grace to accept what is given and faith to trust that you can sustain me.

When I remember the joys of times gone by, help me to thank you for your mercy, which has brought me to the present.

When I am frustrated by the people who are closest to me, open my eyes to see how they are gifts from you, given to guide me into all truth.

Deliver me from sadness, that I might always hope in you and receive even my suffering as an opportunity to share your redeeming love for a broken world.

Lord Jesus Christ, Son of God, have mercy on me, a sinner.

Against Anger

Once again, Lord Jesus Christ, I face the power of anger.

Against the torrent of oblivion, I plead the blood of Jesus.

When I am harmed by another, or think myself to have been, give me patience to go to that person with a humble spirit, seeking to be reconciled.

When I am outraged by injustice, show me clearly how I too must repent of complicity in this world's broken systems, and cover me in your mercy.

When I can neither rest nor work because of the indignation that stirs my spirit, teach me the power of forgiveness and the freedom of love.

Deliver me from anger, that I might not be consumed by its fire but turn the great energy of my soul toward a desire to serve you and your little ones.

Lord Jesus Christ, Son of God, have mercy on me, a sinner.

Against a Lack of Care

Once again, Lord Jesus Christ, I face the power of acedia.

Against the torrent of oblivion, I plead the blood of Jesus.

When the day stretches out before me and I am tempted to despair, encourage my soul through rhythms of prayer and work.

When I imagine my life would be easier if only I were somewhere else, help me not to flee but to trust your grace in this place.

When I lack attentive care for my neighbor, remind me how you laid down your life for me when I was still an enemy.

Deliver me from acedia, that I might greet that of you in every person and know the place where I am standing to be holy ground.

Lord Jesus Christ, Son of God, have mercy on me, a sinner.

Against Vainglory

Once again, Lord Jesus Christ, I face the power of vainglory.

Against the torrent of oblivion, I plead the blood of Jesus.

When I am praised for the good you have done in me, help me to praise your goodness and to remember the sin that keeps me from praising you without ceasing.

When I long for others to know how much I am suffering for you, humble me before the cross and overwhelm my spirit with your unsurpassable love.

When I imagine the great things I might do for you, give me small things to do by the power of your great love, and grant me strength to do them.

Deliver me from vainglory, that I might not be handed over to pride or sadness but ascend by your little way to the humility in which my joy may be complete.

Lord Jesus Christ, Son of God, have mercy on me, a sinner.

Against Pride

Once again, Lord Jesus Christ, I face the power of pride.

Against the torrent of oblivion, I plead the blood of Jesus.

When I am tempted to turn your good gifts into my own achievements, teach me to pray, "My help comes from the Lord."

When I imagine my discernment is superior to your clear commandments, grant me faith to trust your word, which cannot fail.

When the opinions of my sisters and brothers seem simpleminded, help me to recall how you spoke to Balaam through his donkey, and if you should choose to speak through me, help me remember the same.

Deliver me from pride, that I might submit my twisted will to yours and grow up into the fullness of the divine image that you stamped on bodies made from clay.

Lord Jesus Christ, Son of God, have mercy on me, a sinner.

✠ For Direction

Lead me from death to life,
from lies to truth.
Lead me from despair to hope,
from fear to trust.

Lead me from hatred to love,
from war to peace.
Let peace fill our hearts, our world,
our universe with peace. Amen.

✦ Major Life Transition

Lord, help me now to unclutter my life, to organize myself in
the direction of simplicity. Lord, teach me to listen to my heart;
teach me to welcome change, instead of fearing it. Lord, I give
you these stirrings inside me. I give you my discontent. I give you
my restlessness. I give you my doubt. I give you my despair. I give
you all the longings I hold inside. Help me to listen to these signs
of change, of growth; help me to listen seriously and follow where
they lead through the breathtaking empty space of an open door.

✦ For Grace to Serve

It was your joy to serve.
Thank you for your service.
Show me where you want me to serve,
give me the ability to serve,
let me serve.
And make my heart pure toward everyone.

It was your joy to sacrifice.
Thank you for your sacrifice.
Show me what you want me to sacrifice,
give me the ability to sacrifice,
let me sacrifice.
And make my heart pure toward everyone.

It was your joy to suffer.
Thank you for your suffering.
Show me how you want me to suffer,

give me the ability to suffer,
let me suffer.
And make my heart pure toward everyone.

✠ When Walking with Grief

Do not hurry as you walk with grief;
it does not help the journey.
Walk slowly, pausing often.
Do not hurry as you walk with grief.
Be not disturbed by memories that come unbidden.
Swiftly forgive, and let Christ speak for you unspoken words.
Unfinished conversation will be resolved in him.
Be not disturbed.
Be gentle with the one who walks with grief.
If it is you, be gentle with yourself.
Swiftly forgive; walk slowly, pausing often.
Take time; be gentle as you walk with grief.

✠ Before or After a Meal

Lord God, Creator of All,
in your wisdom,
you have bound us together so that we must depend on others
for the food we eat,
the resources we use,
the gifts of your creation that bring life, health, and joy.

Creator God, we give thanks.

Holy be the hands that sew our clothes so that we do not have to
go naked.
Sacred be the hands that build our homes so that we do not have
to be cold.

Blessed be the hands that work the land so that we do not have to go hungry.

Creator God, we give thanks.

Holy be the feet of all who labor so that we might have rest.
Sacred be the feet of all who run swiftly to stand with the oppressed.
Blessed be the feet of all whose bodies are too broken or weary to stand.

Creator God, we give thanks.

Holy be the sound of children laughing to take away our sorrow.
Sacred be the sound of water falling to take away our thirst.
Blessed be the sound of your people singing to heal our troubled hearts.

Creator God, we give thanks.

Holy be the bodies of those who know hunger.
Sacred be the bodies of those who are broken.
Blessed be the bodies of those who suffer.
In your mercy and grace,
soften our callous hearts
and fill us with gratitude for all the gifts you have given us.
In your love,
break down the walls that separate us
and guide us along your path of peace,
that we might humbly worship you in Spirit and in truth.
Amen.

✣ To Welcome the Sabbath

Lord of Creation,
create in us a new rhythm of life
composed of hours that sustain rather than stress,
of days that deliver rather than destroy,
of time that tickles rather than tackles.

Lord of Liberation,
by the rhythm of your truth, set us free
from the bondage and baggage that break us,
from the Pharaohs and fellows who fail us,
from the plans and pursuits that prey upon us.

Lord of Resurrection,
may we be raised into the rhythm of your new life,
dead to deceitful calendars,
dead to fleeting friend requests,
dead to the empty peace of our accomplishments.

To our packed-full planners, we bid, "Peace!"
To our over-caffeinated consciences, we say, "Cease!"
To our suffocating selves, Lord, grant release.

Drowning in a sea of deadlines and death chimes,
we rest in you, our lifeline.

By your ever-restful grace,
allow us to enter your Sabbath rest
as your Sabbath rest enters into us.

In the name of our Creator,
our Liberator,
our Resurrection and Life,
we pray.
Amen.

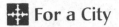 **For a City**

Almighty God,
we praise you for all you have done.
Help us with all that you want us to do.

Come, Holy Creator,
and rebuild the city of (*name*)
so that we do not labor in vain without you.

Come, Holy Savior,
and heal all that is broken
in our lives and in our streets.

Come, Holy Spirit,
and inspire us with the energy and willingness
to rebuild (*name*) to your honor and glory.

Amen.*

---

*This prayer was adapted from the "Prayer for Camden" created by Sacred Heart Parish in Camden, New Jersey.

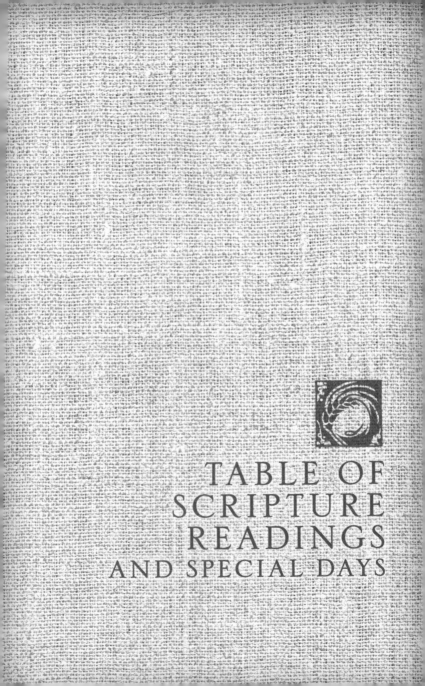

TABLE OF
SCRIPTURE
READINGS
AND SPECIAL DAYS

To find each day's Scripture readings for the morning office, consult the following table. (For the days of Holy Week, use the table on p. 103.) This table also indicates special days that occur in each month. For information regarding the person or event commemorated on a special day, consult the "Annotated List of Special Days" (pp. 105–51).

Date	Special Day	Psalm	OT	NT
12-1	Charles de Foucauld	Ps 8:4-7	Isa 1:1-9	Lk 20:1-8
12-2	Martyrs of El Salvador	Ps 12:1-5	Isa 1:10-20	Lk 20:9-18
12-3		Ps 18:3-7	Isa 1:21-31	Lk 20:19-26
12-4		Ps 22:22-25	Isa 2:1-11	Lk 20:27-40
12-5		Ps 27:1-4	Isa 2:12-22	Lk 20:41-21:4
12-6	Nicholas of Myra	Ps 33:18-21	Isa 3:8-15	Lk 21:5-19
12-7	Ambrose of Milan	Ps 37:1-4	Isa 4:2-6	Lk 7:28-35
12-8		Ps 41:1-3,13	Isa 5:1-7	Lk 21:20-28
12-9	Martin de Porres	Ps 48:2-7	Isa 5:8-12, 18-23	Lk 21:29-38
12-10	Thomas Merton	Ps 54:1-6	Isa 5:13-17, 24-25	Lk 22:1-13
12-11	El Mozote Massacre	Ps 59:1-5	Isa 6:1-13	Lk 22:14-30
12-12		Ps 65:5-8	Isa 7:1-9	Lk 22:31-38
12-13		Ps 69:6-7, 14-15	Isa 7:10-25	Lk 22:39-53
12-14	John of the Cross	Ps 73:14-18	Isa 8:1-15	Lk 22:54-69
12-15		Ps 78:40-43	Isa 8:16-9:1	Mt 3:1-12
12-16		Ps 82:1-5	Isa 9:1-7	Mt 11:2-15
12-17		Ps 89:14-18	Isa 9:8-17	Jn 3:16-21
12-18	Slavery Abolished in the US	Ps 96:9-13	Isa 9:18-10:4	Jn 5:30-47

Date	Special Day	Psalm	OT	NT
12-19		Ps 101:1–4	Isa 10:5–19	Lk 1:5–25
12-20		Ps 104:32–37	Isa 10:20–27	Lk 1:26–38
12-21		Ps 106:1–5	Isa 11:1–9	Lk 1:39–56
12-22		Ps 109:20–25	Isa 11:10–16	Lk 1:57–66
12-23		Ps 115:9–13	Isa 28:9–22	Lk 1:67–80
12-24	Christmas Eve	Ps 118:19–24	Isa 59:15b–21	Php 2:5–11
12-25	Christmas	Ps 119:89–93	Zec 2:10–13	Lk 2:1–14
12-26	Stephen of Jerusalem	Ps 119:164–68	Isa 62:6–7, 10–12	Jn 3:31–36
12-27		Ps 128	Isa 65:15b–25	Lk 4:14–21
12-28	Holy Innocents	Ps 136:1–3, 23–25	Jer 31:15–17	Mt 2:13–18
12-29		Ps 143:7–11	Isa 12:1–6	Jn 7:37–52
12-30		Ps 147:1–5	Isa 25:1–9	Jn 7:53–8:11
12-31	Watch Night	Ps 150	Isa 26:1–9	Jn 8:12–19
1-1	Quaker Jubilee	Ps 7:7–12	Ge 12:1–7	Jn 16:23b–30
1-2	Basil of Caesarea	Ps 14:1–4	Ge 28:10–22	Jn 6:41–47
1-3	Martin Luther	Ps 18:29–32	Ex 3:1–12	Jn 6:35–42, 48–51
1-4		Ps 23	Jos 1:1–9	Jn 10:7–17
1-5		Ps 28:6–9	Isa 66:18–23	Jn 14:6–14
1-6	Epiphany	Ps 33:1–6	Isa 60:1–6,9	Mt 2:1–12
1-7		Ps 37:36–39	Ge 1:1–2:3	Gal 1:1–17
1-8		Ps 42:1–3, 6–7	Ge 2:4–25	Gal 1:18–2:10
1-9		Ps 47:5–8	Ge 3:1–24	Gal 2:11–21
1-10		Ps 55:1–6	Ge 4:1–16	Gal 3:1–14
1-11	Brother Lawrence	Ps 61:4–8	Ge 4:17–26	Gal 3:15–22
1-12	Gandhi's Fast for Peace	Ps 67:1–4	Ge 6:1–8	Gal 3:23–29

Date	Special Day	Psalm	OT	NT
1–13	Moratorium on Death Penalty	Ps 70	Ge 6:9–22	Gal 4:1–11
1–14		Ps 73:24–29	Ge 7:1–10, 17–23	Gal 4:12–20
1–15	Martin Luther King Day	Ps 78:1–3, 12–14	Ge 8:6–22	Gal 4:21–31
1–16	Salvadoran Peace Accord	Ps 85:1–4	Ge 9:18–29	Gal 5:1–15
1–17	Anthony of Egypt	Ps 89:47–52	Ge 11:1–9	Gal 5:16–24
1–18	Hawaii Occupied	Ps 94:1–4	Ge 11:27–12:8	Gal 5:25–6:10
1–19		Ps 98:1–4	Ge 12:9–13:1	Gal 6:11–18
1–20		Ps 104:2–6	Ge 13:2–18	Eph 1:1–14
1–21		Ps 106:6–12	Ge 14:1–24	Eph 1:15–23
1–22	*Roe v. Wade*	Ps 107:33–38	Ge 15:1–11, 17–21	Eph 2:1–10
1–23		Ps 114	Ge 16:1–14	Eph 2:11–22
1–24	California Gold Rush	Ps 119:25–28	Ge 16:15–17:14	Eph 3:1–13
1–25		Ps 119:73–76	Ge 17:15–27	Eph 3:14–21
1–26		Ps 119:108–12	Ge 18:1–16	Eph 4:1–16
1–27		Ps 126:1–4	Ge 18:16–33	Eph 4:17–32
1–28		Ps 138:1–5	Ge 19:1–29	Eph 5:1–14
1–29		Ps 139:13–16	Ge 21:1–21	Eph 5:15–33
1–30	Gandhi Assassinated	Ps 146:4–8	Ge 22:1–18	Eph 6:1–9
1–31	Marcella of Rome	Ps 147:6–9	Ge 23:1–20	Eph 6:10–24
2–1	Brigid of Ireland	Ps 1:1–3	Ge 24:1–27	Jn 13:1–20
2–2	The Presentation of Christ	Ps 10:15–19	Mal 3:1–4	Lk 2:22–40
2–3		Ps 18:26–28	Ge 24:28–38, 49–51	Jn 13:21–30

Date	Special Day	Psalm	OT	NT
2-4	Rosa Parks	Ps 20:5-8	Ge 24:28-38, 49-51	Jn 13:31-38
2-5	First Sit-In	Ps 27:15-18	Ge 24:50-67	Jn 14:1-7
2-6		Ps 33:13-17	Ge 25:19-34	Jn 14:8-17
2-7	Dom Helder Camara of Recife	Ps 37:5-9	Ge 26:1-6, 12-33	Jn 14:18-31
2-8	Dawes Act	Ps 39:5-8	Ge 27:1-29	Jn 15:1-11
2-9		Ps 49:15-19	Ge 27:30-45	Jn 15:12-27
2-10	Nelson Mandela	Ps 50:1-3,6	Ge 27:46-28:4,10-22	Jn 16:1-15
2-11		Ps 59:11-14	Ge 29:1-20	Jn 16:16-33
2-12	NAACP	Ps 66:4-8	Ge 29:20-35	Jn 17:1-11
2-13	Apology to Australia's Aboriginees	Ps 69:20-23	Ge 30:1-24	Jn 17:12-19
2-14	Valentine of Rome	Ps 72:16-19	Ge 31:1-24	Jn 17:20-26
2-15		Ps 78:69-72	Ge 31:25-50	Heb 7:1-28
2-16	Kyoto Protocol	Ps 84:2-6	Ge 32:3-21	Heb 8:1-13
2-17		Ps 89:1-5	Ge 32:22-33:17	Heb 9:1-14
2-18	Hagar the Egyptian	Ps 94:21-23	Ge 35:1-20	Heb 9:15-28
2-19	Japanese Internment	Ps 95:8-11	Ge 37:1-11	Heb 10:1-10
2-20	Frederick Douglass	Ps 104:25-31	Ge 37:12-24	Heb 10:11-25
2-21	Malcolm X	Ps 105:1-3; 106:47-48	Ge 37:25-36	Heb 10:26-39
2-22		Ps 108:2-6	Ge 39:1-23	Heb 11:1-12
2-23	Polycarp of Smyrna	Ps 115:1-4	Ge 40:1-23	Heb 11:13-22
2-24		Ps 119:17-20	Ge 41:1-13	Heb 11:23-31

Date	Special Day	Psalm	OT	NT
2-25	Hebron Massacre	Ps 119:101-4	Ge 41:14-45	Heb 11:32-12:2
2-26		Ps 119:169-72	Ge 41:46-57	Heb 12:3-11
2-27	Constantine	Ps 127:1-4	Ge 42:1-17	Heb 12:12-29
2-28		Ps 138:7-9	Ge 42:18-28	Heb 13:1-16
2-29		Ps 142:1-4	Ge 42:29-38	Heb 13:17-25
3-1		Ps 6:6-9	Ge 43:1-15	Mk 1:1-13
3-2		Ps 13	Ge 43:16-34	Mk 1:14-28
3-3	Mexican/Chicano Student Walkout	Ps 18:14-18	Ge 44:1-17	Mk 1:29-45
3-4		Ps 22:1-6	Ge 44:18-34	Mk 2:1-12
3-5		Ps 28:1-4	Ge 45:1-15	Mk 2:13-22
3-6		Ps 32:6-8	Ge 45:16-28	Mk 2:23-3:6
3-7	Perpetua and Felicity	Ps 37:19-22	Ge 46:1-7, 28-34	Mk 3:7-19a
3-8		Ps 43:1-4	Ge 47:1-26	Mk 3:19b-35
3-9		Ps 49:4-8	Ge 47:27-48:7	Mk 4:1-20
3-10		Ps 55:22-24	Ge 48:8-22	Mk 4:21-34
3-11		Ps 60:1-4	Ge 49:1-28	Mk 4:35-41
3-12	Maximilian of Thavaste / Rutilio Grande Murdered	Ps 66:14-18	Ge 49:29-50:14	Mk 5:1-20
3-13		Ps 69:1-5	Ge 50:15-26	Mk 5:21-43
3-14		Ps 74:17-20	Ex 1:6-22	Mk 6:1-13
3-15		Ps 78:34-39	Ex 2:1-22	Mk 6:13-29
3-16	Rachel Corrie	Ps 84:8-12	Ex 2:23-3:15	Mk 6:30-46
3-17	Patrick of Ireland	Ps 89:34-37	Ex 3:16-4:12	Mk 6:47-56
3-18	Cyril of Jerusalem	Ps 93:4-6	Ex 4:10-31	Mk 7:1-23
3-19	Iraq War	Ps 99:1-5	Ex 5:1-6:1	Mk 7:24-37
3-20		Ps 104:1,13-16	Ex 7:8-24	Mk 8:1-10

Date	Special Day	Psalm	OT	NT
3-21	Sharpeville Massacre	Ps 106:47-48	Ex 7:25-8:19	Mk 8:11-26
3-22		Ps 109:29-30	Ex 9:13-35	Mk 8:27-9:1
3-23		Ps 115:14-18	Ex 10:21-11:8	Mk 9:2-13
3-24	Oscar Romero	Ps 119:34-37	Ex 12:1-14	Mk 9:14-29
3-25	The Annunciation	Ps 119:141-44	Isa 7:10-14	Lk 1:26-38
3-26	Harriet Tubman	Ps 119:153-56	Ex 12:14-27	Mk 9:30-41
3-27		Ps 130	Ex 12:28-39	Mk 9:42-50
3-28	Amos the Prophet	Ps 133	Ex 12:40-51	Mk 10:1-16
3-29		Ps 141:1-3	Ex 13:3-10	Mk 10:17-31
3-30		Ps 146:1-3	Ex 13:1-2, 11-16	Mk 10:32-45
3-31		Ps 148:7-13	Ex 13:17-14:4	Mk 10:46-52
4-1		Ps 1:1-3,6	Ex 14:5-22	1Jn 1:1-10
4-2		Ps 9:1-3,9-10	Ex 14:21-31	1Jn 2:1-11
4-3		Ps 16:5-9	Ex 15:1-21	1Jn 2:12-17
4-4	Martin Luther King Jr.	Ps 20:1-4, 6-7	Ex 15:22-16:10	1Jn 2:18-29
4-5		Ps 24:1-6	Ex 16:10-21	1Jn 3:1-10
4-6		Ps 30:1-3, 12-13	Ex 16:22-36	1Jn 3:11-18
4-7	Rwandan Genocide	Ps 35:1,24-28	Ex 17:1-16	1Jn 3:19-4:6
4-8		Ps 38:1-2, 14-15,21-22	Ex 18:1-12	1Jn 4:7-21
4-9	Dietrich Bonhoeffer	Ps 44:1-2, 9-10,22,25-26	Ex 18:13-27	1Jn 5:1-12
4-10	William Booth	Ps 50:1-3,6	Ex 19:1-16	1Jn 5:13-21
4-11		Ps 56:1-2, 11-12	Ex 19:16-25	2Jn 1-13
4-12		Ps 62:1-3, 13-14	Ex 20:1-21	3Jn 1-13

Date	Special Day	Psalm	OT	NT
4-13		Ps 68:4-6, 24-26,36	Ex 24:1-18	1Th 1:1-10
4-14	Kateri Tekakwitha	Ps 71:1-3, 15-17	Ex 25:1-22	1Th 2:1-12
4-15		Ps 75:1-2, 7-10	Ex 28:1-4, 30-38	1Th 2:13-20
4-16		Ps 79:1,9-13	Ex 32:1-20	1Th 3:1-13
4-17	Bay of Pigs Invasion	Ps 86:3-5, 11-13	Ex 32:21-34	1Th 4:1-12
4-18		Ps 90:1-4,12	Ex 33:1-23	1Th 4:13-18
4-19		Ps 96:1-4, 11-13	Ex 34:1-9	1Th 5:1-11
4-20		Ps 102:1-4	Ex 34:10-17	1Th 5:12-28
4-21		Ps 105:1-2, 8-11	Ex 34:18-35	2Th 1:1-12
4-22	Earth Day	Ps 107:1-3, 8-9	Ex 40:18-38	2Th 2:1-12
4-23	Cesar Chavez	Ps 110:1-5	Lev 16:1-19	2Th 2:13-17
4-24		Ps 116:1-4	Lev 16:20-34	2Th 3:1-18
4-25		Ps 119:33-38	Lev 19:1-18	1Pe 1:1-12
4-26	Chernobyl Disaster	Ps 119:105-8, 111-12	Lev 19:26-37	1Pe 1:13-25
4-27	Rally for the Disappeared	Ps 120:1-3, 6-7	Lev 23:1-22	1Pe 2:1-10
4-28		Ps 133	Lev 23:23-44	1Pe 2:11-25
4-29		Ps 139:1,6-9	Lev 25:1-17	1Pe 3:13-4:6
4-30	End of the Vietnam War	Ps 144:1-2, 13-16	Lev 25:35-55	1Pe 4:7-19
5-1	International Workers' Day	Ps 2:1-2, 11-13	Lev 26:1-20	Lk 3:1-14
5-2		Ps 10:1-3, 10-11	Lev 26:27-42	Lk 3:15-22

Date	Special Day	Psalm	OT	NT
5-3	Septima Poinsette Clark	Ps 15	Nu 3:1–13	Lk 4:1–13
5-4		Ps 19:1–4	Nu 6:22–27	Lk 4:14–30
5-5		Ps 25:1–5	Nu 10:29–36	Lk 4:31–37
5-6		Ps 30:4–7	Nu 11:1–23	Lk 4:38–44
5-7		Ps 36:1–4	Nu 11:24–33	Lk 5:1–11
5-8		Ps 39:5–8	Nu 12:1–6	Lk 5:12–26
5-9	Columba of Iona	Ps 45:1–4	Nu 13:1–3, 21–30	Lk 5:27–39
5-10	Isidore the Farmer	Ps 51:11–13	Nu 13:31–14:25	Lk 6:1–11
5-11		Ps 57:6–10	Nu 14:26–45	Lk 6:12–26
5-12		Ps 63:1–4	Nu 16:1–19	Lk 6:27–38
5-13	Julian of Norwich	Ps 67:1–4	Nu 16:20–35	Lk 6:39–49
5-14	Brother Juniper	Ps 72:1–2, 12–14	Nu 16:36–50	Lk 7:1–17
5-15	International Conscientious Objectors' Day / Al Nakba	Ps 76:1–4	Nu 17:1–11	Lk 7:18–35
5-16	Denmark Bans Slave Trade	Ps 80:4–7	Nu 20:1–13	Lk 7:36–50
5-17	Catonsville Nine	Ps 86:6–10	Nu 20:14–29	Lk 8:1–15
5-18	Origen of Alexandria	Ps 92:1–4	Nu 21:4–9, 21–35	Lk 8:16–25
5-19		Ps 95:1–5	Nu 22:1–21	Lk 8:26–39
5-20	East Timor's Independence Day	Ps 103:1–5	Nu 22:21–38	Lk 8:40–56
5-21		Ps 105:24, 42–45	Nu 22:41–23:12	Lk 9:1–17
5-22	Trail of Tears	Ps 109:20–25	Nu 23:11–26	Lk 9:18–27
5-23		Ps 111:1–2, 9–10	Nu 24:1–13	Lk 9:28–36

Date	Special Day	Psalm	OT	NT
5-24		Ps 117	Nu 24:12-25	Lk 9:37-50
5-25		Ps 119:44-48	Nu 27:12-23	Lk 9:51-62
5-26		Ps 119:114-17	Nu 32:1-6, 16-27	Lk 10:1-17
5-27	Rahab	Ps 121:1-3, 7-8	Jos 2:1-21	Lk 10:17-24
5-28		Ps 132:8-13	Nu 35:1-3, 9-15,30-34	Lk 10:25-37
5-29	Poor People's Campaign	Ps 140:4-6	Dt 1:1-18	Lk 10:38-42
5-30		Ps 144:3-8	Dt 3:18-28	Lk 11:1-13
5-31	Feast of the Visitation	Ps 149:1-4	Zep 3:14-18a	Lk 1:39-49
6-1		Ps 3:1-5	Dt 4:1-9	Ac 1:1-14
6-2	First Mother's Day	Ps 11:1-6	Dt 4:9-14	Ac 1:15-26
6-3		Ps 17:1-3,8-9	Dt 4:15-24	Ac 2:1-21
6-4	Tiananmen Square Massacre	Ps 21:8-14	Dt 4:25-31	Ac 2:22-36
6-5	Six-Day War	Ps 26:8-12	Dt 5:1-22	Ac 2:37-47
6-6		Ps 32:1-7	Dt 5:22-33	Ac 4:32-5:11
6-7	Seattle	Ps 36:5-10	Dt 11:1-12	Ac 5:12-26
6-8		Ps 39:11-15	Dt 11:13-19	Ac 5:27-42
6-9		Ps 46:1-4	Dt 12:1-12	Ac 6:1-15
6-10		Ps 52:1-5	Dt 13:1-11	Ac 6:15-7:16
6-11		Ps 58:3-8	Dt 16:18-20;17:14-20	Ac 7:17-29
6-12		Ps 64:1-4, 8-10	Dt 26:1-11	Ac 7:30-43
6-13		Ps 70:1-6	Dt 29:2-15	Ac 7:44-8:1a
6-14	Gilbert Keith Chesterton	Ps 73:1-6	Dt 29:16-29	Ac 8:1-13

Date	Special Day	Psalm	OT	NT
6-15	Civil Defense Drill Protest	Ps 78:1–4	Dt 30:1–10	Ac 8:14–25
6-16	Soweto Massacre	Ps 81:1–5	Dt 30:11–20	Ac 8:26–40
6-17	John Wesley	Ps 88:15–19	Dt 31:30–32:14	Ac 9:1–9
6-18		Ps 91:1–4	Ru 1:1–18	Ac 9:10–19a
6-19	Juneteenth	Ps 97:1–3, 10–12	Ru 1:19–2:13	Ac 9:19b–31
6-20	Osanna of Mantua	Ps 104:32–37	Ru 2:14–23	Ac 9:32–43
6-21	Freedom Summer Campaign Murders	Ps 106:8–12	Ru 3:1–18	Ac 10:1–16
6-22		Ps 108:1–4	Ru 4:1–17	Ac 10:17–33
6-23		Ps 112:1–3, 9–10	Eze 33:1–11	Ac 10:34–48
6-24		Ps 118:19–24	Eze 33:21–33	Ac 11:1–18
6-25	United Nations Charter	Ps 119:41–44, 48	Eze 34:1–16	Ac 11:19–30
6-26		Ps 119:131–36	Eze 34:17–24	Ac 12:1–17
6-27		Ps 122:1–5	Eze 37:1–14	Ac 12:18–25
6-28	Irenaeus of Lyon	Ps 134	Eze 37:15–28	Ac 13:1–12
6-29	Peter and Paul	Ps 141:1,3–6	Eze 39:21–29	Ac 13:13–25
6-30		Ps 145:1–4	Eze 47:1–12	Ac 13:26–43
7-1		Ps 4:1–3	Jdg 2:1–5, 11–23	Ac 13:44–52
7-2		Ps 12:1–2,5–6	Jdg 3:12–30	Ac 14:1–18
7-3		Ps 18:1–3, 18–20	Jdg 4:4–23	Ac 14:19–28
7-4	Martin of Tours	Ps 22:22–25	Jdg 5:1–18	Ac 15:1–21
7-5		Ps 27:1–4	Jdg 5:19–31	Ac 15:22–35

Date	Special Day	Psalm	OT	NT
7-6	Jan Hus	Ps 33:12-15	Jdg 6:1-24	Ac 15:36-16:5
7-7		Ps 37:7-10	Jdg 6:25-40	Ac 16:16-40
7-8		Ps 41:1-3	Jdg 7:1-18	Ac 17:1-15
7-9	Ruling on the Israeli Wall	Ps 47:6-10	Jdg 7:19-8:12	Ac 17:16-34
7-10	Toyohiko Kagawa	Ps 53:1-3,6	Jdg 8:22-35	Ac 18:1-11
7-11	Benedict of Nursia	Ps 59:10-12, 15	Jdg 9:1-16, 19-21	Ac 18:12-28
7-12		Ps 65:4-7	Jdg 9:22-25, 50-57	Ac 19:1-20
7-13		Ps 69:1-3,18	Jdg 11:1-11, 29-40	Ac 19:21-41
7-14		Ps 74:1-3,9	Jdg 12:1-7	Ac 20:1-16
7-15		Ps 77:14-16, 19-20	Jdg 13:1-24	Ac 20:17-38
7-16		Ps 82:1-4	Jdg 14:1-19	Ac 21:1-14
7-17		Ps 89:1-2,18	Jdg 14:20-15:20	Ac 21:15-36
7-18		Ps 93:1-3	Jdg 16:1-14	Ac 21:37-22:16
7-19	First Women's Rights Convention	Ps 98:6-10	Jdg 16:15-31	Ac 22:17-29
7-20		Ps 104:1, 10-12	Jdg 17:1-13	Ac 22:30-23:11
7-21		Ps 106:47-48	Jdg 18:1-15	Ac 23:12-24
7-22	Mary Magdalene	Ps 109:1-3	Jdg 18:16-31	Ac 23:23-35
7-23		Ps 113:1-3,8	1Sa 1:1-20	Ac 24:1-23
7-24		Ps 119:1-5	1Sa 1:21-2:11	Ac 24:24-25:12
7-25	Invasion of Puerto Rico	Ps 119:53-56	1Sa 2:12-26	Ac 25:13-27

Date	Special Day	Psalm	OT	NT
7-26	Americans with Disabilities Act	Ps 119:121–25	1Sa 2:27–36	Ac 26:1–23
7-27		Ps 123	1Sa 3:1–12	Ac 26:24–27:8
7-28		Ps 135:1–2, 15–18	1Sa 9:1–14	Ac 27:9–26
7-29		Ps 142:1–2, 5–7	1Sa 9:15–10:1	Ac 27:27–44
7-30	William Wilberforce	Ps 144:9–11	1Sa 10:1–16	Ac 28:1–16
7-31	Ignatius of Loyola	Ps 145:5–9	1Sa 10:17–27	Ac 28:17–31
8-1		Ps 5:1–4	1Sa 11:1–15	Mt 25:1–13
8-2	Basil the Blessed	Ps 13:3–6	1Sa 12:1–6, 16–25	Mt 25:14–30
8-3		Ps 18:6–11	1Sa 13:5–18	Mt 25:31–46
8-4		Ps 23	1Sa 13:19–14:15	Mt 26:1–16
8-5	Atmospheric Test Ban Treaty	Ps 27:5–9	1Sa 14:16–45	Mt 26:17–25
8-6	The Transfiguration / Bombing of Hiroshima	Ps 99:5–9	Ex 34:29–35	Lk 9:28–36
8-7		Ps 37:1–6	1Sa 15:1–3, 7–23	Mt 26:26–35
8-8		Ps 40:1–6	1Sa 15:24–35	Mt 26:36–46
8-9	Franz Jägerstätter	Ps 46:5–10	1Sa 16:1–13	Mt 26:47–56
8-10		Ps 54	1Sa 16:14–17:11	Mt 26:57–68
8-11	Clare of Assisi	Ps 57:1–5	1Sa 17:17–30	Mt 26:69–75
8-12		Ps 66:1–4	1Sa 17:31–49	Mt 27:1–10
8-13	Integration of Little Rock High School	Ps 69:34–38	1Sa 20:1–23	Mt 27:11–23

Date	Special Day	Psalm	OT	NT
8-14	Maximilian Kolbe	Ps 71:4-8	1Sa 20:24-42	Mt 27:24-31
8-15		Ps 77:1-4	1Sa 24:1-22	Mt 27:32-44
8-16	Solidarity in Poland	Ps 80:1-3	1Sa 25:1-22	Mt 27:45-54
8-17		Ps 88:1-6	1Sa 25:23-44	Mt 27:55-66
8-18		Ps 92:5-8	1Sa 28:3-20	Mt 28:1-10
8-19		Ps 97:5-9	1Sa 31:1-13	Mt 28:11-20
8-20		Ps 102:25-28	2Sa 1:1-16	Ro 8:1-11
8-21	Nat Turner's Slave Revolt	Ps 105:3-7	2Sa 2:1-11	Ro 8:12-25
8-22		Ps 107:33-35,41-43	2Sa 5:1-12	Ro 8:26-30
8-23		Ps 113:4-7	2Sa 7:1-17	Ro 8:31-39
8-24		Ps 116:14-17	2Sa 7:18-29	Ro 9:1-18
8-25		Ps 119:49-52	2Sa 9:1-13	Ro 9:19-33
8-26	Women's Suffrage	Ps 119:137-38,142-44	2Sa 11:1-27	Ro 10:1-13
8-27		Ps 122:6-9	2Sa 12:1-14	Ro 10:14-21
8-28	Augustine of Hippo	Ps 132:14-19	2Sa 12:15-31	Ro 11:1-12
8-29	John the Baptist	Ps 143:4-8	2Sa 18:9-33	Ro 11:13-24
8-30	Mississippi Freedom Democratic Party	Ps 145:14-18	2Sa 23:1-7, 13-17	Ro 11:25-36
8-31		Ps 146:1-3	2Sa 24:1-2, 10-25	Ro 12:1-8
9-1		Ps 6:1-4	Est 1:1-4, 10-19	Mt 4:18-25
9-2		Ps 9:13-15, 19-20	Est 2:5-8, 15-23	Mt 5:1-10
9-3		Ps 16:1-4	Est 3:1-4:3	Mt 5:11-16

Date	Special Day	Psalm	OT	NT
9-4		Ps 19:7-10	Est 4:4-17	Mt 5:17-20
9-5		Ps 24:7-10	Est 5:1-14	Mt 5:21-26
9-6		Ps 31:21-24	Est 6:1-14	Mt 5:27-37
9-7		Ps 37:11-14	Est 7:1-10	Mt 5:38-48
9-8	United Farm Workers Union	Ps 43:1-4	Est 8:1-8, 15-17	Mt 6:1-6, 16-18
9-9	Peter Claver	Ps 44:15-18	Hos 1:1-2:1	Mt 6:7-15
9-10	Mother Teresa of Calcutta	Ps 51:16-20	Hos 2:2-14	Mt 6:19-24
9-11	1973 Chilean Coup / 2001 Terrorist Attacks	Ps 56:3-7	Hos 2:14-23	Mt 6:25-34
9-12	Armenian Genocide in Turkey	Ps 64:1,5-7	Hos 3:1-5	Mt 7:1-12
9-13	Attica Prison Revolt / Oslo Accords	Ps 69:16-17, 21-23	Hos 4:1-10	Mt 7:13-21
9-14	John Chrysostom	Ps 71:19-23	Hos 4:11-19	Mt 7:22-29
9-15	Bombing of Sixteenth Street Baptist Church	Ps 77:5-10	Hos 5:1-7	Mt 8:1-17
9-16		Ps 80:14-17	Hos 5:8-6:6	Mt 8:18-27
9-17	Hildegard of Bingen	Ps 89:5-8	Hos 10:1-15	Mt 8:28-34
9-18		Ps 90:14-17	Hos 11:1-19	Mt 9:1-8
9-19		Ps 95:8-11	Hos 13:4-14	Mt 9:9-17
9-20	Paul Chong Hasang	Ps 103:8-13	Hos 14:1-9	Mt 9:18-26
9-21	Henri Nouwen	Ps 105:12-15	Mic 1:1-9	Mt 9:27-34
9-22		Ps 107:4-8	Mic 2:1-13	Mt 9:35-10:15
9-23		Ps 112:4-8	Mic 3:1-8	Mt 10:16-42

Date	Special Day	Psalm	OT	NT
9-24		Ps 116:5-8	Mic 3:9-4:5	Mt 11:1-15
9-25		Ps 119:57-63	Mic 5:1-4, 10-15	Mt 11:16-30
9-26		Ps 119:146-52	Mic 6:1-8	Mt 12:1-14
9-27	Vincent de Paul	Ps 128:1-6	Mic 7:1-7	Mt 12:15-21
9-28		Ps 135:3-7	Jnh 1:1-17a	Mt 12:22-32
9-29		Ps 139:2-5	Jnh 1:17-2:10	Mt 12:33-42
9-30		Ps 145:10-13	Jnh 3:1-4:11	Mt 12:43-50
10-1	Therese of Lisieux	Ps 4:4-8	Jer 35:1-19	Jas 1:1-15
10-2		Ps 10:12-19	Jer 36:1-10	Jas 1:16-27
10-3		Ps 17:13-16	Jer 36:11-26	Jas 2:1-13
10-4	Francis of Assisi	Ps 22:26-30	Jer 36:27-37:2	Jas 2:14-26
10-5		Ps 25:6-10	Jer 37:3-21	Jas 3:1-12
10-6	Fannie Lou Hamer	Ps 33:1-5	Jer 38:1-13	Jas 3:13-4:12
10-7	Afghan War	Ps 35:17-23	Jer 38:14-28	Jas 4:13-5:6
10-8		Ps 40:12-14	2Ki 25:8-12, 22-26	Jas 5:7-12
10-9	Oskar Schindler	Ps 46:9-12	Jer 29:1,4-14	Jas 5:13-20
10-10	Women in Black	Ps 55:18-20, 24-26	Jer 44:1-14	2Co 1:1-11
10-11		Ps 59:1-5	La 1:1-12	2Co 1:12-22
10-12	"Indigenous Peoples Day"	Ps 62:6-9	La 2:8-15	2Co 1:23-2:17
10-13		Ps 68:7-10	Ezr 1:1-11	2Co 3:1-18
10-14		Ps 72:1-7	Ezr 3:1-13	2Co 4:1-12
10-15	Teresa of Avila	Ps 81:13-16	Ezr 4:7,11-24	2Co 4:13-5:10
10-16	Cuban Missile Crisis	Ps 85:7-11	Hag 1:1-2:9	2Co 5:11-6:2

Date	Special Day	Psalm	OT	NT
10-17	Ignatius of Antioch	Ps 89:11-15	Zec 1:7-17	2Co 6:3-13
10-18		Ps 91:9-13	Ezr 5:1-17	2Co 6:14-7:1
10-19	John Woolman	Ps 96:7-10	Ezr 6:1-22	2Co 7:2-16
10-20		Ps 102:13-16	Ne 1:1-11	2Co 8:1-16
10-21		Ps 106:1-5	Ne 2:1-20	2Co 8:16-24
10-22		Ps 109:28-30	Ne 4:1-23	2Co 9:1-15
10-23		Ps 115:12-18	Ne 5:1-19	2Co 10:1-18
10-24		Ps 118:6-9	Ne 6:1-19	2Co 11:1-21a
10-25		Ps 119:73-77	Ne 12:27-31a,42b-47	2Co 11:21b-33
10-26		Ps 119:153-56	Ne 13:4-22	2Co 12:1-10
10-27		Ps 124:1-5	Ezr 7:1-26	2Co 12:11-21
10-28		Ps 135:13-14, 19-21	Ezr 9:1-15	2Co 13:1-14
10-29	Clarence Jordan	Ps 140:1-3, 7-9	Ezr 10:1-17	Tit 1:1-16
10-30		Ps 145:19-22	Ne 9:1-38	Tit 2:1-3:15
10-31		Ps 146:4-9	Ne 7:73b-8:3,5-18	Phm 1-25
11-1	All Saints	Ps 8	Rev 7:2-4, 9-17	Mt 5:1-12
11-2	World Christian Gathering of Indigenous People	Ps 9:16-20	Joel 1:1-13	Rev 8:1-13
11-3	Martin de Porres	Ps 18:21-25	Joel 1:15-20	Rev 9:1-12
11-4	Watchman Nee	Ps 22:12-17	Joel 2:1-11	Rev 9:13-21
11-5		Ps 25:11-14	Joel 2:12-19	Rev 10:1-11
11-6		Ps 31:9-12	Joel 2:21-27	Rev 11:1-14
11-7		Ps 37:19-21, 28-29	Joel 2:28-3:8	Rev 11:14-19

Date	Special Day	Psalm	OT	NT
11-8		Ps 40:7-11	Joel 3:9-17	Rev 12:1-6
11-9	Fall of the Berlin Wall	Ps 44:3-7	Hab 1:1-2:1	Rev 12:7-17
11-10	Kristallnacht	Ps 51:1-4	Hab 2:1-4, 9-20	Rev 13:1-10
11-11	Armistice Day	Ps 60:1-5	Hab 3:1-18	Rev 13:11-18
11-12		Ps 66:14-18	Mal 1:1,6-14	Rev 14:1-13
11-13		Ps 68:28-34	Mal 2:1-16	Rev 14:14-15:8
11-14		Ps 73:12-18	Mal 3:1-12	Rev 16:1-11
11-15		Ps 78:18-22	Mal 3:13-4:6	Rev 16:12-21
11-16		Ps 81:8-12	Zec 9:9-16	Rev 17:1-18
11-17		Ps 86:14-17	Zec 10:1-12	Rev 18:1-14
11-18		Ps 94:12-15	Zec 11:4-17	Rev 18:15-24
11-19		Ps 98:1-5	Zec 12:1-10	Rev 19:1-10
11-20		Ps 102:17-22	Zec 13:1-9	Rev 19:11-21
11-21		Ps 106:43-46	Zec 14:1-11	Rev 20:1-6
11-22	Eberhard and Emmy Arnold	Ps 107:10-16	Zec 14:12-21	Rev 20:7-15
11-23		Ps 115:1-3, 9-11	Isa 65:17-25	Rev 21:1-8
11-24		Ps 118:1-5	Isa 19:19-25	Rev 21:22-22:5
11-25		Ps 119:65-68	Na 1:1-13	Rev 22:6-13
11-26	Sojourner Truth	Ps 119:169-74	Ob 15-21	Rev 22:14-21
11-27		Ps 125	Zep 3:1-13	Mk 13:1-8
11-28		Ps 136:1-3, 7-9	Isa 24:14-23	Mk 13:9-23
11-29	Dorothy Day	Ps 139:10-16	Mic 7:1-10	Mk 13:24-31
11-30		Ps 147:1-5	Mic 7:11-20	Mk 13:32-37

Day of Holy Week	Psalm	OT	NT
Palm Sunday	Ps 118:25–29	Zec 9:9–17	Lk 19:29–40
Monday	Ps 36:5–10	Isa 42:1–9	Mk 14:3–9
Tuesday	Ps 71:1–3,9–12	Isa 49:1–6	Mk 11:15–19
Wednesday	Ps 69:8–15	Isa 50:4–9a	Mt 26:1–5,14–25
Maundy Thursday	Ps 78:14–17	Ex 12:1–14a	Jn 13:1–15
Good Friday	Ps 22:1–2,9–11	Ge 22:1–18	Jn 19:1–37
Holy Saturday	Ps 31:1–5	Job 14:1–14	Jn 19:38–42
Easter Sunday	Ps 114	Ex 14:10–15:1	Mt 28:1–10

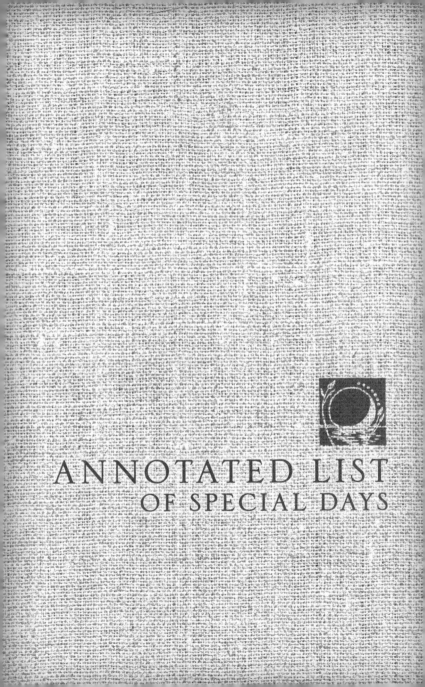

ANNOTATED LIST
OF SPECIAL DAYS

December 1: Charles de Foucauld (1858 – 1916). While working in the North African desert after a dishonorable discharge from military service, Charles de Foucauld was impressed by the piety of Muslims and experienced a dramatic recovery of his Christian faith. He spent a number of years in a Trappist monastery before hearing the call to a new monasticism among the working poor. "I no longer want a monastery which is too secure," he wrote. "I want a small monastery, like the house of a poor workman who is not sure if tomorrow he will find work and bread, who with all his being shares the suffering of the world." Though Foucauld died in solitude, the Little Brothers and Sisters of Jesus, inspired by his life and witness, have started communities of service among the poor and outcast around the world.

December 2: Martyrs of El Salvador. In 1980, Maura Clarke, Ita Ford, Dorothy Kazel, and Jean Donovan were murdered by officers of the Salvadoran military. Missionaries serving among the poor during El Salvador's civil war, these women knew, as Ita Ford said the night before she died, that "one who is committed to the poor must risk the same fate as the poor." Their deaths affected the North American church deeply, galvanizing opposition to US support for the Salvadoran government's repression of its people.

December 6: Nicholas of Myra (Fourth Century). The original "Old St. Nick" who inspired the tradition of Santa Claus, Nicholas was bishop of Myra in fourth-century Turkey. Little is known about his life except that he entrusted himself to Jesus at an early age and, when his parents died, gave all of their possessions to the poor. While serving as bishop, Nicholas learned of three girls who were going to be sold into slavery by their father. Moved to use the church's wealth to ransom the lives of these little ones, he tossed three bags of gold through the family's window. We recall this ancient Christmas gift, even as we remember that 1.2 million children are trafficked each year in the global sex trade today.

December 7: Ambrose of Milan (339 – 397). A provincial governor in fourth-century Italy, Ambrose was drafted to serve as bishop before he was even baptized. At first reluctant to serve the church, he finally accepted the call and took the task seriously. Ambrose gave away all of his possessions, took up a strict schedule of daily prayer, and committed himself to the study of Scripture. Called from the world of politics to serve the church, Ambrose was a leader who spoke truth to power and did not back down, insisting that "the emperor is in the church, not over it."

December 9: Martin de Porres (1579 – 1639). Martin de Porres was a Dominican brother who is often celebrated by mixed-race people and those committed to ending racism and segregation. He was born in Lima, Peru, the son of a Spanish nobleman and a former slave from Panama. Having grown up familiar with poverty and prejudice, he became a passionate advocate for those on the margins, establishing an orphanage and hospital for children, and becoming well known for his compassion. Martin is often depicted with a broom because he considered all work to be sacred and was committed to service and sacrifice.

December 10: Thomas Merton (1915 – 1968). Thomas Merton pursued the ideals of pleasure and freedom in early adulthood only to reject them as an illusion and embrace a life of prayer and silence as a Trappist monk. His 1949 conversion story, *The Seven Storey Mountain*, was a surprise bestseller, introducing millions of modern people to the gifts of monasticism. A mentor to many activists in the Catholic peace movement, Merton became a prophetic voice for peace and nonviolence in the twentieth century, despite the fact that his "political" writings were censored by his order. Convinced that contemplative life must engage the world, he prepared the way for a new monasticism.

December 11: El Mozote Massacre. In 1981, scores of Salvadoran troops from the US-trained Atlacatl Battalion occupied the town of El Mozote in rural El Salvador, interrogating its citizens about the whereabouts of guerilla troops suspected to be in the area. Though the residents of El Mozote, many of them born-again evangelicals, were known to be neutral in the conflict between the Salvadoran government and the FMLN (Farabundo Marti National Liberation Front) resistance, nearly one thousand men, women, and children were systematically killed in the largest massacre in modern Latin American history.

December 14: John of the Cross (1542 – 1591). Born into poverty in sixteenth-century Spain, Juan de la Cruz joined the Carmelite order at the age of twenty-one. Four years later, he met Teresa of Avila, who was impressed by the young friar and recruited him to help her restore a spirit of radical simplicity to the Carmelites. Their reforms were not welcomed in the days of Spain's Inquisition, and Juan suffered a great deal of persecution at the hands of his religious brothers. One of the great mystics of the Christian tradition, he teaches us how to draw closer to God during the "dark night of the soul."

December 18: Slavery Abolished in the US. With the passing of the thirteenth amendment to the Constitution of the United States of America, slavery was abolished in the US on December 18, 1865.

December 26: Stephen of Jerusalem (? – 35). Stephen was the first in a long line of Christian martyrs. He looked on those who were about to kill him and asked the Lord to forgive them (Acts 7:60). His courageous nonviolence in the face of death resembled that of Christ. It is said that Jesus sat at the Father's side after his ascension into heaven, but rose to greet Stephen when he arrived.

December 28: Holy Innocents. Matthew's gospel records that after Jesus was born, King Herod was so disturbed by the news of a potential contender for the throne that he ordered a preemptive strike, executing all boys in Bethlehem who were under two years of age. Since its earliest centuries, the church has remembered these "holy innocents" who died because Jesus' coming posed a threat to those in power. Today, we remember all the little ones, born and unborn, who are sacrificed in a culture of death that has not yet welcomed the good news of Jesus. And we recall that Herod's kingdom is now long gone, but the kingdom of God goes on.

December 31: Watch Night. Established in African-American communities on December 31, 1862, Watch Night is a gathering to celebrate the Emancipation Proclamation becoming law. When the clock struck midnight on January 1, 1863, all slaves in the Confederate States were proclaimed free. Since that date 146 years ago, African-Americans have celebrated the good news of freedom in local churches on New Year's Eve. Like the slaves who first gathered while the Civil War raged on, we proclaim freedom for all captives in Jesus' name, knowing that for millions, freedom is not a reality. Our celebration is a commitment to join modern-day slaves and undocumented workers in their struggle for justice.

January 1: Quaker Jubilee. In 1788, Quakers in Pennsylvania freed their slaves, anticipating the emancipation of chattel slaves in the United States that occurred some seventy-five years later. Together with free blacks, abolitionist evangelicals, and slaves who were willing to risk their lives, Quakers led one of America's most vibrant faith-based justice movements — the Underground Railroad. Committed to simplicity, religious freedom, and nonviolence, Quakers have contributed to movements for peace and justice throughout US history.

January 2: Basil of Caesarea (330 – 379). Basil was born in what is now Turkey. His grandfather was martyred, and his brother Gregory of Nyssa became an influential bishop. In an age marked by doctrinal battles within the church, Basil was a tireless defender of orthodoxy. He is known as an early developer of Christian monasticism and an incredible preacher and writer.

Among his many writings are some of the church's earliest prayers. Basil left the world to join the monastery, but eventually brought the monastery to the world through the city of Basiliad, also called "The New City." This giant community of monastic men and women worked with doctors and other laypeople to provide food, clothing, shelter, and medical assistance to the poor of Caesarea. Basil later became a priest and a bishop, but he always kept his vision of a monastic life not cut off from the world but embracing the pain and sorrow of the world.

January 3: Martin Luther. Martin Luther, an Augustinian monk and biblical scholar, wrote against the church's use of indulgences and insisted that salvation is a free gift from God, not achieved through good works. Luther refused to recant his criticism of the church, saying, "Here I stand. I cannot do otherwise." He was excommunicated by Pope Leo X on January 3, 1521, unwittingly becoming the leader of a movement that later was named the Great Reformation.

January 6: Epiphany. *Epiphany* means "to make manifest." By the fourth century, Epiphany was a major annual celebration for the church. On this day, Jesus' divine mission is revealed when the magi visit him, and we remember his baptism, miracles, and ministry, as well as his call for us to follow him.

January 11: Brother Lawrence (1611 – 1691). Born Nicholas Herman in Lorraine, France, Brother Lawrence received little formal education and, as a young man, served briefly in the army. One day, he had an experience that set the course of his life in a new direction. Gazing at a barren tree in winter, Lawrence saw for the first time the majesty of God's grace and the constancy of God's providence. He imagined himself like the tree, waiting for the life that God inevitably brings in due season. Shortly after this experience, he became a lay brother in the Carmelite monastery in Paris. There he worked in the kitchen and, in the repetition of his daily chores, found a way to integrate spirituality and work, which he called the "practice of the presence of God." By learning to perform his mundane tasks for the sake of God, Brother Lawrence turned every moment into an opportunity for prayer.

January 12: Gandhi's Fast for Peace. On January 12, 1948, Mohandas Gandhi began his last successful fast in New Delhi to convince Hindus and Muslims in the city to work toward peace. Six days later, convinced that harmony was achieved, he ended the fast. For most of his adult life, Gandhi read Jesus' Sermon on the Mount every morning, convinced that it contained a truth more powerful than the empire that occupied his native India or the enmity that divided Hindus and Muslims. Through "experiments in truth" like the public fast, he sought to put Jesus' teachings into practice for the sake of peace.

January 13: Moratorium on the Death Penalty. In 2003, George Ryan, Republican governor of Illinois, called for a moratorium on the death penalty. Persuaded by the work of law students exposing race and class discrimination in the handing down of death sentences, he called for a halt on executions. Though his political career was tainted by scandal, the 2003 moratorium affirmed and fueled the fire of Christians and other abolitionists working for restorative justice and an end to the death penalty.

January 15: Martin Luther King Day. On January 15, 1929, Martin Luther King Jr. was born in Atlanta, Georgia. In 1983, celebrating his contribution to the civil rights movement, the United States Congress made the third Monday in January a national holiday. While we celebrate Dr. King's contribution to America, we also remember his insistence that the church exist as the "conscience of the state," speaking prophetically to those in power. We honor Dr. King with all Americans, and we remember that the sermon he intended to preach the Sunday after his assassination was titled "Why America May Go to Hell."

January 16: Salvadoran Peace Accord. After twelve years of civil war and approximately seventy-five thousand deaths,

El Salvador's government and rebel leaders signed a peace treaty in Mexico City on January 16, 1992. Six government negotiators, five guerilla commanders, and five rebel negotiators signed the treaty, one after another.

January 17: Anthony of Egypt (251 – 356). Anthony was born in Egypt in the middle of the third century and lost his parents at a young age, inheriting a fair amount of land and wealth. Soon after, when he heard a gospel reading in church exhorting the rich man to "go, sell your possessions and give to the poor," he did just that, vowing to dedicate his life to God. Anthony lived for a time in his native city, pursuing prayerful asceticism. After fifteen years, at the age of thirty-five, he withdrew to the solitude of the desert and began his monastic life of prayer, study, and work. After many years of living in the desert, Anthony remained whole and healthy, and he radiated compassion and joy. He lived to the age of 105 and is remembered as the father of the church's first monastic movement.

January 18: Hawaii Occupied. In 1893, Lorrin Thurston, the grandson of Christian missionaries, convinced President Benjamin Harrison of the urgent need to annex Hawaii to protect American lives and property. When US troops arrived on Hawaiian soil, Queen Liliuokalani surrendered her throne to prevent bloodshed. One hundred years later, President Bill Clinton apologized to Native Hawaiians, calling the overthrow of Hawaii's monarchy an illegal act.

January 22: *Roe v. Wade*. On January 22, 1973, the United States Supreme Court decided in *Roe v. Wade* that a mother has the legal right to end her pregnancy until the point at which the fetus can live outside of her womb. We lament the death of each child lost to abortion. We pray for each parent who has chosen to terminate a pregnancy. And we commit to become a people who welcome life in a culture of death.

January 24: California Gold Rush. On January 24, 1848, James Marshall discovered gold in the American River, setting off the California Gold Rush. Prior to the discovery of this precious metal, one hundred and fifty thousand Native Americans lived in California. White settlers in search of gold brought with them genocide through disease and violence. In 1851, the government of California endorsed the extermination of Native people. In some cases paying five dollars per head, they invested a million dollars in the systematic murder of men, women, and children. By 1870, only an estimated thirty-one thousand California Natives had survived.

January 30: Gandhi Assassinated (1948). While walking to evening prayer in New Delhi, India, Mohandas Gandhi was shot five times at point-blank range and died almost immediately. Gandhi was the primary political and spiritual leader of India during his country's independence movement. He was one of the first in India to practice mass civil disobedience and nonviolent protest against the tyranny in his country, inspiring a host of twentieth-century activists.

January 31: Marcella of Rome (325 – 410). Marcella had an enviable life as the daughter of a prominent Roman family and the wife of a wealthy man. But less than a year after her wedding, her husband died. She could have continued living in luxury when the wealthy consul Cerealis proposed to her. She chose instead to convert her mansion into one of the earliest communities of women, where she and other noblewomen used their riches to help the poor. Marcella said she preferred to "store her money in the stomachs of the needy than hide it in a purse." In 410, during their invasion of Rome, Goths broke into Marcella's house. When they demanded money, she calmly responded that she had no riches because she had given all to the poor. Though she was an elderly woman, they beat her and tortured her mercilessly. Her attackers eventually were shamed by her piety and released her, but she died a short time later.

February 1: Brigid of Ireland (c. 450 – 525). It is believed that Brigid was the daughter of a pagan Scottish king and a Christian Pictish slave. Even as a child, she was known to have a generous spirit and a compassionate, tender heart, and she was drawn to help the poor, the hungry, and the cold. Eventually, Brigid's father decided she had to be married or taken into someone else's household, because he could no longer afford to keep her (especially because of her excessive giving to the poor, which he feared would be the ruin of him). Brigid refused marriage and became a nun with seven other women. At Kildare, she founded a double monastery for monks and nuns, assisted by a bishop. The perpetual fire at the monastery became a symbol of its hospitality and constant, undying devotion to God and the poor.

February 2: The Presentation of Christ in the Temple. On February 2, the church remembers Jesus' presentation in the temple in Jerusalem. Along with their newborn son, Mary and Joseph brought a sacrifice of two pigeons, the offering permitted in the law of Moses for those too poor to afford a lamb (Lev. 12:8). Despite their lack of wealth, these peasants from Galilee carried in their arms the salvation of the whole world. Simeon and Anna, a holy man and a devout woman of Israel, immediately recognized the incalculable value of the present they had brought. We sing "Simeon's Song" (see Saturday in "Evening Prayer" in the full edition of *Common Prayer*) to train our eyes to see the salvation of the world in the presents of the poor.

February 4: Rosa Parks. Rosa Parks was born February 4, 1913. When she was forty-two, Parks refused to give up her seat on a city bus in Montgomery, Alabama, to a white passenger, which at the time, the law required of African-Americans. She was arrested for her act of civil disobedience and worked with others from the NAACP to start the Montgomery Bus Boycott. The resulting integration of city buses in Montgomery ignited the civil rights movement in the United States and inspired nonviolent movements for social change around the world.

February 5: First Sit-In. On February 1, 1960, four college students — Ezell A. Blair Jr., David Richmond, Joseph McNeil, and Franklin McCain — initiated the first sit-in demonstration at a Woolworth's lunch counter in Greensboro, North Carolina. The store manager ignored the protestors, hoping they would leave. The next day, twenty-seven more students came to protest. By February 5, three hundred students had arrived, igniting a mass movement of sit-ins for desegregation throughout the South.

February 7: Dom Helder Camara of Recife (1909 – 1999). Dom Helder Camara, born February 7, 1909, in Fortazela, Brazil, became a bishop of the Catholic Church and one of the twentieth century's great apostles of nonviolence. After joining a conservative political movement as a young priest, Camara experienced a conversion while ministering among the poor in the favelas of Rio de Janeiro. "When I fed the poor, they called me saint," Camara said. "When I asked why they were poor, they called me a communist." Labeled "the red bishop," Camara worked tirelessly for democracy and human rights in Brazil, even as he watched friends and fellow priests be imprisoned, tortured, and killed. Once, when the elderly Camara answered a knock on his door, the hired assassin he found on his doorstep was so moved by the sight of him that he blurted out, "I can't kill you. You are one of the Lord's."

February 8: Dawes Act. On February 8, 1887, the Dawes Act was approved by the United States Congress, dividing Native American reservation lands into properties to be owned and maintained by individuals, both Native and white. Tribes were to be dissolved and Native Americans were expected to assimilate into white American culture. Most of the land granted to individual Native Americans was desert, unable to sustain agriculture.

February 10: Nelson Mandela. On February 10, 1990, Nelson Mandela was released after spending twenty-seven years in a South African prison. He had been sentenced to life imprisonment for plotting to overthrow his government as part of the African National Congress (AFM), which opposed the apartheid policies of the ruling National Party. While imprisoned, he became one of the most influential black leaders of South Africa. After the apartheid policy was defeated through nonviolent struggle, Mandela became South Africa's first black president.

February 12: NAACP. The National Association for the Advancement of Colored People (NAACP) was established on February 12, 1909, after a race riot in Springfield, Illinois. Some of the founding members were W. E. B. DuBois, Ida Wells-Barnett, and Oswald Garrison Villard. It became one of the most influential justice organizations in the United States, leading movements against lynching, segregation, discrimination, and racial violence.

February 13: Apology to Australia's Aboriginees. On February 13, 2008, the prime minister of Australia, Kevin Rudd, issued a national apology to aboriginal families torn apart by Australian government agencies and church missions during the period between 1869 and 1969. During this time, children were taken from their families and forced into institutions, where they often were not allowed to speak their native language and were given new names and birthdates. It is estimated that between 1910 and 1971, fifty-five thousand children were taken from their families.

February 14: Valentine of Rome (d. 269). A Christian priest in Rome, Valentine was known for assisting Christians persecuted under Claudius II. After being caught marrying Christian couples and helping Christians escape persecution, Valentine was arrested and imprisoned. Although Emperor Claudius originally liked Valentine, the priest was condemned to death when he tried to convert the emperor. Valentine was beaten with stones, clubbed, and, finally, beheaded on February 14, 269. In the year 496, February 14 was designated a day of celebration in Valentine's honor. He has since become the patron saint of engaged couples, beekeepers, happy marriages, lovers, travelers, young people, and greetings.

February 16: Kyoto Protocol. On February 16, 2005, the Kyoto Protocol went into effect as an international attempt to reduce greenhouse gases and slow global warming. The protocol places more responsibility on developed countries because they are responsible for the highest levels of greenhouse gas emissions.

February 18: Hagar the Egyptian. When Abraham's wife, Sarah, was unable to have a child, she gave Abraham her Egyptian slave, Hagar, as a wife. Sarah was following ancient surrogate customs, which allowed a wife to give her maid to her husband and then claim the child as her own. But after Hagar conceived a son by Abraham, Sarah became bitter and resentful and treated her harshly. Hagar's response was to run away into the wilderness, but an angel of the Lord appeared to Hagar and urged her to return and submit to her mistress. The Lord directed Hagar to call the child Ishmael (which means "God hears") and, as he did Abraham, promised her descendants so numerous they could not be counted. Hagar called God *El-roi* — "the God who sees" — and was struck with awe that she had seen him.

February 19: Japanese Internment. On February 19, 1942, following the bombing of Pearl Harbor by Japanese warplanes the previous December, President Franklin Roosevelt signed an executive order calling for the displacement of one hundred and twenty thousand Japanese Americans to internment camps.

February 20: Frederick Douglass (1818 – 1895). Frederick Douglass was born a slave in Maryland. His mother died shortly after his birth, and he was raised by his grandparents. A resourceful youth, he learned how to read and write by giving away food in exchange for reading lessons from neighborhood kids. Before long, he was able to teach other slaves to read the

Bible through weekly Sunday schools. In 1838, at the age of twenty, Douglass escaped from slavery by impersonating a sailor and went on to become one of the most famous abolitionists and leaders in US history. He was a firm believer in the equality of all people, whether black, female, Native American, or recent immigrant. He was fond of saying, "I would unite with anybody to do right and with nobody to do wrong."

February 21: Malcolm X. On February 21, 1965, Malcolm X was assassinated while delivering a speech in Manhattan's Audubon Ballroom. Malcolm X became a well-known advocate for civil rights after joining the Nation of Islam while in prison. A brilliant, self-educated leader, Malcolm experienced multiple conversions, eventually leaving the Nation of Islam after a pilgrimage to Mecca and committing to overcome racism through an international solidarity movement. Though he was not a Christian, Malcolm X spoke prophetically about the church's complicity in Western culture's sin of racism.

February 23: Polycarp of Smyrna (70 – 155). Polycarp was arrested by Roman officials after having served as bishop of Smyrna for many decades. When the Roman proconsul ordered him to declare that "Caesar is Lord" and to curse Christ, the elderly Polycarp refused, saying, "Eighty-six years I have served him and he never did me any wrong. How can I blaspheme my King, who saved me?" Polycarp was sentenced to death by fire, but the flames miraculously stood like a wall around him and he was not burned. The executioner then stabbed him in the heart, which issued such an abundance of blood that the fire was quenched.

February 25: Hebron Massacre. On this day in 1994, a Jewish settler from New York entered the Ibrahimi Mosque in Hebron with an automatic weapon and killed twenty-nine Muslims during prayer, which has become known as the Hebron Massacre. This massacre has been a landmark in the conflict in the Middle East, which is so often fueled by religious extremists reacting to other religious extremists. It is a reminder that extremists of all faiths have distorted the best that our faiths have to offer, and it is our prayer that a new generation of extremists for love and grace will rise up.

February 27: Constantine. In the year 280, Roman Emperor Constantine was baptized into the church, beginning Christianity's transition from a minority movement to an empire's religion. It was not long before the persecuted became the persecutors, and the cross of Christ was exchanged for the sword of Rome.

March 3: Mexican/Chicano Student Walkout. On March 3, 1968, more than twenty thousand Mexican and Chicano students walked out of Los Angeles high schools, calling for an end to racist policies. The students had not been allowed to speak Spanish in the classroom or to use the bathroom during lunchtime. Mexican-American history was often denied, and Chicano students were being advised toward menial labor instead of college.

March 7: Perpetua and Felicity (d. 203). The relationship between Perpetua and Felicity began as that of a noblewoman and her servant girl. But when they embraced Christ, they became sisters in faith and ultimately co-martyrs. In 203 AD, Roman authorities arrested six Christians and condemned them to death by the sword for refusing to renounce their faith. Among these six were twenty-two-year-old Perpetua, who had a young child, and her former slave, Felicity, who was eight months pregnant. Felicity gave birth while in prison, the night before their execution date, and her child was entrusted to a Christian couple. Eyewitness accounts document that just before their deaths, the two women, now equals in Christ, embraced one another with a holy kiss.

March 12: Maximilian of Thavaste (d. 295)/Rutilio Grande Murdered. Maximilian, the son of a Roman soldier in what is now Algeria, was required to join the army at the age of twenty-one. Before the court of the Roman proconsul Dion,

Maximilian testified, "I cannot enlist, for I am a Christian. I cannot serve, I cannot do evil." Because of his refusal, he was beheaded. Also noteworthy: this is the day that Jesuit priest Rutilio Grande was murdered in El Salvador, a pivotal moment in Salvadoran history and in the witness of the church in Latin America.

March 16: Rachel Corrie. Twenty-three-year-old American activist Rachel Corrie was killed on this day in 2003. While countless Palestinian people have been killed the way Rachel was, her death marks a key moment symbolizing international concern. She was crushed by a bulldozer in Gaza as she knelt in front of the home of a Palestinian friend and tried to stop the demolition of her house.

March 17: Patrick of Ireland (389 – 461). At the age of sixteen, Patrick was kidnapped by Irish marauders and taken to Ireland, where he was sold as a slave to a chieftain and forced to herd livestock. After six years of slavery, Patrick escaped to his native Britain. Because he believed that his captivity and deliverance were ordained by God, Patrick devoted his life to ministry. While studying for the priesthood, he experienced recurring dreams in which he heard voices say, "O holy youth, come back to Erin and walk once more amongst us." He convinced his superiors to let him return to Ireland in 432, not to seek revenge for injustice but to seek reconciliation and to spread his faith. Over the next thirty years, Patrick established churches and monastic communities across Ireland. When he was not engaged in the work of spreading the Christian faith, Patrick spent his time praying in his favorite places of solitude and retreat.

March 18: Cyril of Jerusalem (315 – 386). Cyril lived in the fourth century. His gift to the church was his refusal to separate good doctrine from good living, insisting that orthodoxy (right belief) and orthopraxis (right living) must be married. He was accused of selling some gifts from the emperor and giving the money to the poor. Cyril was condemned and forced into exile. He died in 386 at the age of seventy. Of his thirty-five years as a bishop, nearly sixteen were spent in exile.

March 19: Iraq War. On March 19, 2003, US and British troops began a "shock and awe" campaign to overthrow the government of Saddam Hussein, which US intelligence officials accused of possessing weapons of mass destruction (WMDs). Though no WMDs were found in Iraq, a US-sponsored occupation continued, costing thousands of soldiers' lives and billions of US dollars.

March 21: Sharpeville Massacre. Under apartheid law, black South African men over the age of sixteen were required to carry a pass card. The police could arrest anyone found without a card. On March 21, 1960, black South African men planned as an act of civil disobedience to leave their pass cards at home, go to the police station, and ask to be arrested. When the men began their walk to the police station, officers opened fire, killing sixty-nine and injuring hundreds in what has been remembered as the Sharpeville Massacre.

March 24: Oscar Romero (1917 – 1980). Although he began as a conservative archbishop, opposed to the progressive liberation theology that was popular among those seeking to help poor farmers in El Salvador, Oscar Romero was deeply impacted when his friend, a priest, was assassinated as a result of a commitment to social justice. Through weekly homilies on national radio, Romero advocated an end to the repression of the people in El Salvador, thus making himself an enemy of the government and the military. He was not successful in ending the violence: more than seventy-five thousand Salvadorans eventually were killed, one million left the country, and another million were left homeless. Because of his prophetic witness, Romero became a target for assassination. As he was saying Mass on March 24, 1980, he was shot and killed. "A bishop will die," Romero had said, foreseeing his own fate, "but the church of God — the people — will not perish."

March 25: The Annunciation. On March 25 we remember the special role that Mary plays in the redemption of the world and celebrate her example to each of us as disciples of Jesus. When the angel Gabriel visited Mary, she was a teenager in occupied Palestine, as anonymous and apparently insignificant as the billions of people who live and die today in the slums of megacities. But the angel of the Lord called Mary by name and proclaimed that she would carry inside her womb God in the flesh. It is a miracle we remember even as we watch it happening in us: however humble our circumstances, God proposes to live in and through our bodies. As a sign to remind us that anything is possible with our God, we remember that Mary conceived Jesus without the help of any man.

March 26: Harriet Tubman (1820? – 1913). Harriet Tubman was born into slavery in the 1820s. In 1849, she had a vision that compelled her to run away, traveling under cover of night with only the North Star as her guide. Arriving safely in Pennsylvania, she felt like she was in heaven. "I had crossed the line," she wrote. "I was FREE; but there was no one to welcome me to the land of freedom." Tubman committed herself to helping others escape to freedom, guiding at least three hundred fugitive slaves to Canada over the course of fifteen years. To those who traveled under her guidance, she was known as Moses.

March 28: Amos the Prophet. Unlike other Old Testament messengers, Amos was not a professional prophet; he had no special qualifications, nor was he related to any other prophets. He was a peasant farmer and sheep tender called by God for a particular mission. A native of the southern kingdom of Judah, Amos received a commission from God to preach to the people of the northern kingdom of Israel. In the first half of the eighth century BC, during a time of great expansion and prosperity in Israel, Amos spoke out against the economic injustices urban elites visited upon the poor. Rich landowners were acquiring money and land, taking advantage of small farmers and peasants. Although Amos was not wealthy, he was sent to warn the wealthy and invite them back into the good way of God's justice.

April 4: Martin Luther King Jr. (1929 – 1968). Martin Luther King Jr. was a black American preacher who became a civil rights leader, teaching nonviolent resistance to evil, and opposing racism and segregation. Working out of his home in the church, King organized a diverse coalition of people to combat the evils of racism, poverty, and militarism. In many ways, he was a flawed hero, but he was a committed man who died for his faith and for the freedom of his people. It was while he was advocating for sanitation workers that he was killed in Memphis, Tennessee, on April 4, 1968.

April 7: Rwandan Genocide. On April 7, 1994, civil war broke out in Rwanda as Hutu extremists began brutally killing Tutsis and moderate Hutus. Over the next one hundred days, nearly a million people were killed in the worst occurrence of genocide since the Holocaust. An estimated 75 percent of the Tutsis living in Rwanda were murdered.

April 9: Dietrich Bonhoeffer (1906 – 1945). Dietrich Bonhoeffer studied theology in Germany and the United States and pastored a church in London before returning to Germany as a leader of the Confessing Church, which tried to resist Adolf Hitler. Though Bonhoeffer returned to Germany a pacifist, he became a resistance worker and was part of a failed plot to assassinate Hitler. But it was his evasion of the call-up for military service that led to his arrest. Perhaps he died because of his political convictions and not as a Christian martyr, but he would have said that there is no distinction between the two.

April 10: William Booth (1829 – 1912). William Booth was a Methodist preacher in Britain who co-founded the Salvation Army. He was born in Nottingham and ended up living and working among the poor and ostracized with his wife, Catherine. Out of their work on the streets was born the Salvation Army, with its uniforms and discipline. The movement became structured as a quasi-military organization with no physical weaponry but with an army of people passionate about salvation and healing the wounds of our broken world.

April 14: Kateri Tekakwitha (1656 – 1680). Kateri Tekakwitha was born in 1656 in what is now New York. Her mother was Algonquin, a Christian Native, and her father was a non-Christian Mohawk Turtle chief. When Tekakwitha was four years old, a smallpox epidemic killed her parents and her brother, and left her with seriously impaired eyesight and a disfigured face. Inspired by Jesuit missionaries at an early age, Tekakwitha was baptized and assumed the name Kateri, probably in honor of Catherine of Siena. The following year, French conquerers reached her community of Ossernenon and destroyed much of it, burning it to the ground and massacring many of the Natives. Kateri escaped on the St. Lawrence River to a village of Christian Natives, where she dedicated her life to chastity, prayer, and care for the sick. She was the first Native American saint in the Catholic Church and is often called the Lily of the Mohawks, and the Apostle of the Indians.

April 17: Bay of Pigs Invasion. On April 17, 1961, the CIA launched its Bay of Pigs invasion of Cuba, an unsuccessful attempt to overthrow Fidel Castro's Communist government. When President John F. Kennedy recognized this action of his own intelligence agency as an attempt to escalate the Cold War, he refused to send in US troops, saying that he would like to "splinter the CIA in a thousand pieces and scatter it to the wind."

April 22: Earth Day. In the spring of 1970, Gaylord Nelson announced that a demonstration about the environment would happen on April 22. Approximately twenty million people showed up to celebrate the first Earth Day. Since then, environmental concerns such as oil spills, global warming, extinction of wildlife, and pollution have been pushed to the forefront of political agendas and popular concern.

April 23: Cesar Chavez (1927 – 1993). Cesar Chavez was a Latino farmworker in the United States who organized the United Farm Workers Union (UFW). Inspired by a priest who taught him God's desire for social justice, Chavez gave himself to voluntary poverty and a nonviolent struggle on behalf of America's poorest and most exploited workers. "When you sacrifice, you force others to sacrifice," he said. "It's an extremely powerful weapon."

April 26: Chernobyl Disaster. On April 26, 1986, a nuclear power accident in Chernobyl, Ukraine, dispersed large amounts of radioactive debris into the air. The plume drifted over parts of the Soviet Union and Europe, extending as far as Ireland. The most contaminated areas were in Ukraine, Belarus, and Russia, forcing the evacuation and resettlement of 336,000 people. Fifty-six people died; it is estimated that eight hundred thousand others suffered radiation exposure.

April 27: Rally for the Disappeared. On April 27, 1977, mothers of abducted children in Buenos Aires, Argentina, held their first rally for the "disappeared." The mothers organized after losing numerous children during Argentina's Dirty War between 1976 and 1983. Many of the children were tortured and killed during this time. The military claims that nine thousand such children are unaccounted for, while the mothers say it is closer to thirty thousand.

April 30: End of the Vietnam War. North and South Vietnam were reunited on April 30, 1975, bringing an end to the Vietnam War.

May 1: International Workers' Day. On May 1, 1886, one hundred and eighty thousand US workers went on strike to demand an eight-hour workday. Rallies continued until May 3, when a bomb was thrown into a crowd and shots were fired, killing eight policemen and an unknown number of civilians. Ever since this incident, remembered as the Haymarket Massacre, May 1 has been known as International Workers' Day.

May 3: Septima Poinsette Clark (1898 – 1987). Septima Poinsette Clark was born in Charleston, South Carolina, to a father who was an ex-slave and a mother who had been raised in the Caribbean. While her parents had very little formal education, they emphasized the need for Septima to go to school. Though Septima was eligible to teach after completing the eighth grade, her parents and teachers encouraged her to finish high school. After graduating, she took a post as a teacher on Johns Island, off the coast of Charleston. There she began to notice the extreme disparity between the education of African-Americans and that of their white counterparts. This experience stayed with her and fueled her quest for educational reform. An avid social activist during the civil rights era, Septima traveled throughout the South to educate African-Americans about their voting rights. She worked closely with Myles Horton of the Highlander Folk School. Together, they trained many civil rights activist, including Rosa Parks, in nonviolent resistance and local leadership. Although Septima was thrown in jail, threatened, fired from jobs, and falsely accused of wrongdoing, she never turned from her task of working against an unjust educational system. Septima Poinsette Clark has become known as the Grandmother of the Civil Rights Movement.

May 9: Columba of Iona (521 – 597). An Irish prince who chose the monastic life, Columba left Ireland in 563 and settled in Iona in Scotland. He was a large man with a big, resonant singing voice. He was also an excellent scribe and illuminator of manuscripts. A much-loved abbot, he had missionary zeal and great prophetic insight. His faithfulness to the Celtic tradition fueled the spread of vital Christianity throughout Britain and beyond as he planted monastic communities to be hubs of prayer and mission, modeling a radical life of discipleship.

May 10: Isidore the Farmer (1070 – 1130). In March 1622, Rome surprised many people by recognizing Isidore as a saint. He founded no order, nor did he write a single book. He was a simple farmworker who spent his life tilling the land, mostly for the same wealthy landowner. His wife, Maria, bore a son who died in childhood. Isidore knew the hardship, toil, and sorrow that is very familiar to many. He went to worship daily and prayed continuously in the fields, displaying the simple and profound faith shared by campesinos around the globe. It was said that angels could be seen assisting Isidore in the fields as he plowed. Though he had very little wealth, he became known for generosity and hospitality, especially to the stranger or the lonely. He died on May 15, 1130.

May 13: Julian of Norwich (1342 – 1416). Born during a tumultuous period of England's history, Julian witnessed tremendous suffering in her lifetime. At age thirty, when she was seriously ill, Julian received the first of sixteen visions that centered on the crucified Christ. She interpreted her visions to mean that God loves us unconditionally, and she likened Christ to a mother who suffers when her child is hurt. Julian became an anchorite, voluntarily restricting herself to a tiny cell in the church building at Norwich. She lived the rest of her days in almost total isolation so that she could pray for the community and offer spiritual counsel. Her *Showings* has been praised as being among the most important spiritual writings in the English language.

May 14: Brother Juniper (d. 1258). A companion of Francis of Assisi, Brother Juniper is remembered as a "fool for Christ," and there are all sorts of wild stories about his antics. He was notorious for constantly giving his possessions away and living with a winsomeness that sometimes got him into trouble. At one point, he was ordered by a superior not to give away his outer garment to the beggars anymore. But it wasn't long before he met someone in need who asked him for some clothing. He replied, "My superior has told me under obedience not to give my clothing to anyone. But if you pull it off my back, I certainly will not prevent you." Francis is said to have joked about how he wished for a forest of Junipers.

May 15: International Conscientious Objectors' Day/ Al Nakba. On May 15 each year, many people gather for International Conscientious Objectors' Day, holding vigils, protests, seminars, and campaigns to draw attention to conscientious objection. A conscientious objector is someone who refuses to serve in the armed forces or to bear arms in a military conflict. This refusal is based on moral or religious beliefs. It is also noteworthy that May 15 is celebrated as Israel's independence day and lamented by Palestinians as "Al Nakba," which means "the day of catastrophe." We remember on this day conflict in the Middle East. And we also celebrate conscientious objectors known as the Israeli Refuseniks.

May 16: Denmark Bans Slave Trade. On May 16, 1792, Denmark decided that trading human beings is immoral and became the first European country to ban the transportation of slaves. It is also worth noting that this day marks the martyrdom of Dirk Willems. Willems is one of the most celebrated martyrs in the Anabaptist tradition (which includes Mennonites, Brethren, and Amish). He was born in the Netherlands and lived during a tumultuous time in Christendom. He is most famous for escaping from prison and turning around to rescue one of his pursuers, who had fallen through the thin ice of a frozen pond while chasing him. He was burned at the stake on May 16, 1569.

May 17: Catonsville Nine. On May 17, 1968, the Catonsville Nine, which included two Catholic priests, went into the Selective Service offices in Catonsville, Maryland, and burned several hundred draft records in protest against the Vietnam War. They were arrested, tried, and found guilty of destroying government property. After the nine were sentenced, one of the priests, Dan Berrigan, asked the judge if the Lord's Prayer could be recited. All in the courtroom, including the judge and prosecuting attorneys, rose and joined in the prayer.

May 18: Origen of Alexandria (c. 185 – c. 254). The oldest of seven children, Origen was born in Alexandria and witnessed at a very young age the public death of his father, who was martyred during the persecutions in 202. While still in his teens, Origen became a teacher, philosopher, and student of Scripture — and a prolific writer — all the while practicing a strict discipline of prayer, fasting, celibacy, and poverty. Though his self-denial was extreme to the point of abuse and some of his teachings ultimately were considered heretical, Origen is still considered one of the greatest early interpreters of Scripture and Christian doctrine. By helping Christians find meaning in the riches of Scripture, he taught a love for truth, sanctity, and, above all, God.

May 20: East Timor's Indepence Day. In 1976, Indonesia annexed East Timor after the sudden withdrawal of the Portuguese. It is estimated that two hundred thousand Timorese died under brutal Indonesian rule. After years of violence between separatist guerillas and pro-Indonesian paramilitary forces, East Timor gained its independence on May 20, 2002. Today, East Timor is one of the world's poorest countries.

May 22: Trail of Tears. In 1838, four thousand Cherokee died in their forced relocation from their land that the Cherokee called *Nunna daul Isunyi* — "the Trail Where They Cried." The displacement of the Cherokee people resulted from the Indian Removal Act of 1830, which was violently implemented by Andrew Jackson. In 1831, the Choctaw were the first to be uprooted, followed by the Seminole in 1832, the Creek in 1834, the Chickasaw in 1837, and finally the Cherokee in 1838. By 1837, forty-six thousand Native Americans had been removed from their homelands.

May 27: Rahab. Rahab's story is found in the book of Joshua. Rahab was a prostitute who hid Hebrew spies in her home while they were on a reconnaissance mission in Jericho. Fearing the God of Israel more than her own king, Rahab agreed to help the spies if they protected her and her family when God delivered her city to them. Though she is an unlikely saint, Rahab is remembered by the authors of Matthew, Hebrews, and James as a faithful witness and an ancestor of Jesus. Her story is a reminder that in God's story, sinners make the best saints.

May 29: Poor People's Campaign. On May 29, 1968, the Poor People's Campaign arrived in Washington, D.C. The campaign was established to broaden the civil rights movement to include disadvantaged people of all races. The main demonstration was held at the Mall in Washington, D.C., where people camped out in tents called Resurrection City. Seven thousand demonstrators made this tent city their home to bring attention to poverty and injustice.

May 31: Feast of the Visitation. On May 31, the church celebrates Mary's visit with her cousin Elizabeth, after she had learned from the angel Gabriel that she would bear the creator of the universe in her womb. Elizabeth was herself pregnant with John the Baptist at the time, and the gospel account tells us that he leapt for joy inside his mother when Mary greeted her. The joy of these two hosts — Mary and Elizabeth — is a reminder to us of the delight that comes when we practice hospitality, inviting God's movement into our lives.

June 2: First Mother's Day. On June 2, 1872, Julia Ward Howe began the celebration of Mother's Day as a holiday to honor mothers by working for an end to all war.

June 4: Tiananmen Square Massacre. In 1989, crowds of university students filled Tiananmen Square in Beijing to protest their government's oppressive regime. Though they were allowed to gather for weeks, on the night of June 3 and the morning of June 4, the Chinese Army massacred hundreds of peaceful protestors.

June 5: Six-Day War. In 1967, the Six-Day War erupted and lasted from June 5 to June 11. Israel fought neighboring nations Egypt, United Arab Republic, Jordan, and Syria in a historic war that precipitated the ongoing conflict in the Middle East. At the war's end, Israel had seized the Gaza Strip and the Sinai

Peninsula from Egypt, the West Bank and East Jerusalem from Jordan, and the Golan Heights from Syria. The status of these territories and the resulting refugee crisis continue to be central concerns in the ongoing Israeli-Palestinian conflict, raising issues of fairness, entitlement, theology, and international law.

June 7: Seattle (1786? – 1866). Seattle was born in a Suquamish village along the Puget Sound. As a child, he witnessed the arrival of the first white folks in the Northwest. In his early twenties, he was named chief of his tribe and inherited the responsibility of dealing with white settlers. He rejected violent resistance and insisted on peaceful discourse. In 1830, he and many other Natives converted to Christianity. Seattle became a leader committed to integrating his faith with his Native culture and traditions. He eventually was disheartened by the way white settlers treated creation. He died on June 7, 1866, on the Port Madison Reservation near the city which today bears his name.

June 14: Gilbert Keith Chesterton (1874 – 1936). A towering presence, G. K. Chesterton was an excitable and opinionated man who was also blessed with a sense of humor that has much to offer a world polarized by politics. He passionately critiqued liberals and conservatives, and maintained a lively and genuine friendship with George Bernard Shaw, with whom he disagreed on nearly everything. Chesterton set out to rethink the faith, but laughingly compared his quest to a voyager who sets out to find a lost land only to rediscover England. At forty-eight, he converted to Catholicism. Amid very serious discourse, he insisted that despair comes not from being weary of suffering but from being weary of joy. He died on this day, and his epitaph describes him as one who helped restore the world to sanity by exaggerating whatever the world neglects.

June 15: Civil Defense Drill Protest. In 1955, twenty-nine people were arrested in New York City for refusing to participate in a civil defense drill requiring all citizens to take shelter in a simulated nuclear attack. "We refused to take part in the war maneuvers, if you can call them that," wrote Dorothy Day, who was among the pacifist resisters. Civil defense drills were discontinued six years later when the annual protest in City Hall Park drew a crowd of thousands.

June 16: Soweto Massacre. In 1976, seven hundred students were killed in Soweto, South Africa, as they struggled against the forces of apartheid.

June 17: John Wesley (1703 – 1791). Though his studies led him to become an Anglican cleric, John Wesley did not at first have a vibrant spiritual life. While en route to the colony of Georgia as a missionary, his ship lost its mast in a violent storm. Witnessing the Moravian passengers sing and pray peacefully through the storm, Wesley realized that he lacked "the one thing necessary." After his heart was "strangely warmed" in a conversion experience, Wesley became a popular preacher among the working class of England and led the movement now called Methodism. The core of his message was that Christianity is based on the experience of God's grace, which bears fruit through a life of love. Wesley said, "When I have money, I get rid of it quickly, lest it find a way into my heart." He died at the age of eighty-eight, lifting his arms and saying, "The best of all, God is with us."

June 19: Juneteenth. In 1865, slaves in Texas were the last to learn of their emancipation following the defeat of the Confederate States of America. In African-American communities throughout the United States, this good news of liberation is still celebrated as Juneteenth.

June 20: Osanna of Mantua (1449 – 1505). Born to wealthy parents in Mantua, Italy, Osanna Andreasi, at age five, heard the voice of God saying, "Life and death consist in loving God." She was then given a vision of heaven and the Trinity. Tradition has it that Osanna learned to read and write by divine revelation and began studying theology after this vision. Against her parents' wishes, she longed to join the Third Order of Dominicans, but she would have to wait thirty-seven years to complete her vows. Upon the untimely death of her parents, Osanna committed her life to serving Christ and caring for her family of siblings. She was privy to ongoing holy visions and was reputed to have received the stigmata — the wounds of Christ. She spent her life aiding the poor and sick and speaking out boldly against aristocrats who lived lavish lives while others suffered.

June 21: Freedom Summer Campaign Murders. In 1964, civil rights activists James Chaney, Andrew Goodman, and Michael Schwerner were murdered as they participated in the Freedom Summer campaign to register black voters in Mississippi.

June 25: United Nations Charter. In 1945, following the end of the Second World War, fifty countries signed the original charter of the United Nations in San Francisco.

June 28: Irenaeus of Lyon (130 – 200). The first systematic theologian of the church, Irenaeus lived in a time when Christianity was young and fragile. He was appointed bishop of Lyon and combated the dualistic notion that matter and spirit are entirely separate, with matter being wholly corrupt. Irenaeus insisted that there is nothing inherently corrupt in creation but that humans lost their "likeness to God" through the distortion of sin. That likeness was restored, Irenaeus proclaimed, through Christ, the "second Adam," who corrected the story of the first Adam. In a time when so much of Christianity has been reduced to disembodied doctrine and otherworldly sentiment, Irenaeus' voice rings out like a prophet's.

June 29: Peter and Paul. One of the ways we see the wisdom of the early church is in their placing Peter and Paul's saint days together so that they have a shared celebration, thereby making sure that there was no room for division over their leadership. (It may be that the church forgot this wisdom in the Reformation, with Rome claiming Peter's authority and Paul becoming the hero of Protestants.) The early church was quite clear that the first pastor and the first theologian of the faith had to be held in equal respect and in equal balance of authority. One without the other leaves us incomplete and unbalanced.

July 4: Martin of Tours (d. 397). Martin of Tours saw Christ in the face of the poor and in the commitment to nonviolence. He was born in what is now Hungary and as a young man was conscripted into the Roman Army. Martin's conversion to Christianity occurred after he met a beggar seeking alms. Without money to offer the man, Martin tore his own coat in half and gave one part to the beggar. The following night, Martin dreamed of Christ wearing half of his coat. Once Martin was baptized, he resolved to leave the army because Christ called him to nonviolence. His superiors saw his request as cowardice until Martin offered to face the enemy without weapons as a sign of Christian pacifism. Instead, he was put in prison. After he was released, he joined the monastery at Solesmes and eventually served for ten years as bishop of Tours.

July 6: Jan Hus (1372 – 1415). Jan Hus was born in Bohemia (now part of the Czech Republic). He helped launch a vigorous reform of the church in a particularly difficult time in church history known as the Great Schism. Amid highly politicized divisions of God's people, Hus pursued a mystical and evangelical approach, insisting that Christ alone is head of the church. To partisans on both sides, his views seemed idealistic at best, and at worst a dreamy anarchism or heresy. Hus maintained a creative loyalty to the church while challenging its pathologies. He was burned at the stake during the Council of Constance in 1415, and his death helped give birth to the Moravian Church. As he died, he said, "It is better to die well than to live wickedly.... Truth conquers all things."

July 9: Ruling on the Israeli Wall. On July 9, 2004, the International Court of Justice ruled that the wall being built by the Israeli government in the contested Palestinian territories was illegal and should be taken down. The Holy Land continues to be one of the most troubled and segregated regions in the world and has been referred to as the place where "the most sophisticated apartheid system in the world" is practiced.

July 10: Toyohiko Kagawa (1888 – 1960). Toyohiko was a Japanese pacifist, Christian reformer, evangelist, and labor activist. He wrote, spoke, and worked on ways to employ Christian principles in the ordering of society. His vocation to help the poor led him to live among them, and he established schools, hospitals, and churches. He also was an innovator and a critical thinker, in everything from economics and theology to cutting-edge gardening techniques. One of his great lines is, "I read in a book that a man called Christ went about doing good. It is very disconcerting to me that I am so easily satisfied with just going about."

July 11: Benedict of Nursia (c. 480 – c. 547). Benedict was born in the town of Nursia, near Rome. At age twenty, he left home and lived for three years as a hermit in a desolate cave. There he practiced severe asceticism, maturing in both mind and character. Though he had little contact with the outside world, Benedict gained a reputation for his holy life and discipline. Eventually, he was asked to lead a monastery in a remote area near Monte Cassino. Drawing on older rules and the wisdom of experience, Benedict outlined in his rule a simple way of life for monks, centered on praying the daily office, studying Scripture, engaging in common labor for the good of the community, and performing works of charity. His vision of the holy life became the standard for Western monasticism and a model for how to live simply — in health, wholeness, and community.

July 19: First Women's Rights Convention. On July 19, 1848, the first Women's Rights Convention was held in Seneca Falls, New York, sparking a women's movement that challenged both the church and the world with the good news that in Jesus Christ, there is neither male nor female.

July 22: Mary Magdalene. Mary of Magdala was the most prominent of the women from Galilee who accompanied Jesus in his ministry. So devoted to Jesus was Mary that, after his death, she returned to the tomb to clean his body. Finding Jesus alive in the garden, she was sent to proclaim the news of his resurrection to the disciples, thus becoming the "apostle to the Apostles." Although she may not have been acknowledged for her discipleship, Mary stands for all those who proclaim Jesus as the risen Christ, bringing to others his gifts of peace, forgiveness, and justice.

July 25: Invasion of Puerto Rico. In 1898, United States troops invaded Puerto Rico, recolonizing its people after their struggle for independence under Spanish rule. Puerto Ricans were given US citizenship, but in the 1930s, a nationalist movement gained popularity and opposed US assimilation.

July 26: Americans with Disabilities Act. On July 26, 1990, President George Bush signed the world's first civil rights law for people with disabilities. The Americans with Disabilities Act protects equal opportunity for people with disabilities in all areas of life, especially independent living and economic self-sufficiency.

July 30: William Wilberforce (1759 – 1833). William Wilberforce, an evangelical Christian in eighteenth-century England, dedicated his life to abolishing slavery. In 1780, Wilberforce was elected to Parliament. After an experience of spiritual rebirth, Wilberforce found his purpose: to use his political life in the service of God. He believed that there was no evil greater than the institution of slavery. "Let the consequences be what they would," he wrote. "I from this time determined that I would never rest until I had effected its abolition." In 1798, he began his campaign: speaking, circulating flyers and petitions, and introducing bills in Parliament. In 1806, Wilberforce managed to get a bill passed in Parliament that prohibited slavery in all British colonies. By the time Wilberforce died in

1833, Parliament had finally passed a bill that freed all slaves throughout the British Empire.

July 31: Ignatius of Loyola (1491 – 1556). Ignatius was born to a noble Spanish family. As a young man, he joined the military, but a war injury ended his military career. While recuperating, Ignatius became bored and asked for novels about knights and battles. But all that could be found in the castle where he stayed were books on the life of Christ and the saints of the church. Legend has it that Ignatius read these stories in a competitive manner, imagining how he could beat the various saints at practicing the spiritual disciplines. He soon found that his thoughts on the saints left him with more peaceful and satisfied feelings than his daydreams about the noble life he had known before his injury. After his illness, Ignatius began practicing his notions of rivaling the saints, and wrote about his experiences of the Christian disciplines. His scribblings became the spiritual classic *The Spiritual Exercises of Saint Ignatius*, which for centuries Christians have used in the practice of discernment. He eventually founded the Society of Jesus, an order still known widely for a commitment to foreign missions and religious education.

August 2: Basil the Blessed (1464 – 1552). Basil was born into a peasant family near Moscow in the late 1400s. He left home at age sixteen to devote himself to a life of asceticism. He did not have a permanent home but instead walked around barefoot and in rags, exhibiting extraordinary humility in the face of punishment and ridicule. Like an Old Testament prophet, Basil challenged those in power about their treatment of the poor, marginalized, and afflicted. He foretold misfortunes and preached the gospel to all who would listen, including the tsar, Ivan the Terrible, who respected and feared Basil's gift of prophecy. Once, when Basil offered the tsar a piece of raw meat during the lenten season, the tsar rejected it. Basil then boldly and truthfully asked him, "Then why do you drink the blood of men?" noting the tsar's violent behavior toward innocent people.

August 5: Atmospheric Test Ban Treaty. In 1963, the United States, the USSR, and Great Britain signed a treaty banning nuclear testing in the atmosphere. President John F. Kennedy quoted Soviet leader Nikita Khrushchev, saying they both hoped to avoid a nuclear war in which "the survivors would envy the dead."

August 6: The Transfiguration/Bombing of Hiroshima. In 1945, the United States dropped an atomic bomb on Hiroshima, Japan, the first use of a nuclear weapon against people. As we remember the transfiguration of Christ in the mysterious light of glory, we also remember all those who were tragically and senselessly transfigured by the first nuclear blast. May their memory help us to see a way toward peace in our time.

August 9: Franz Jägerstätter (1907 – 1943). Franz Jägerstätter was a humble Catholic peasant born to a poor German farm maid in the small town of Radegund, Upper Austria. In the same small parish, he was baptized and married, and worked as a sexton. Though he was never part of any formal resistance group, Franz was his village's sole conscientious objector to the annexation of Austria to Germany under Hitler. He felt deeply that his Christian faith did not permit him to fight in Hitler's army. Even under pressure by local priests and bishops to conform and serve in the military, Franz would not relent. He was imprisoned and beheaded for refusing to serve in the Nazi army.

August 11: Clare of Assisi (1194 – 1255). Clare Offreduccio was born into Italian nobility in 1194. She ran away from home at the age of eighteen after hearing St. Francis preach on the streets of Assisi. She chose to wed Christ instead of the man her parents desired her to marry. With Francis' help, she founded the Franciscan monastic community of the Order of Poor Ladies (The Poor Clares) at San Damiano. Clare became abbess of the order in 1216 and led the sisters in their commitment to poverty and manual labor. Her mother and sisters later joined her order. As abbess, she fought hard to resist papal orders that the Poor

Clares establish a rule of life. She is often depicted holding a monstrance, symbolizing her use of the blessed sacrament to defend her convent from invaders.

August 13: Integration of Little Rock High School. In 1957, following the Supreme Court's decision against racial segregation in *Brown v. Board of Education*, African-American students in Arkansas were admitted to Little Rock High School for the first time.

August 14: Maximilian Kolbe (1894 – 1941). Maximilian Kolbe was a Polish priest who provided shelter for thousands of Jews in his friary and was an active voice against Nazi violence. He was arrested by the German Gestapo and imprisoned at Auschwitz. When a fellow prisoner escaped from the camp, the Nazis selected ten other prisoners to be killed in reprisal. As they were lined up to die, one of the ten began to cry, "My wife! My children! I will never see them again!" At this, Maximilian stepped forward and asked to die in his place. His request was granted, and he led the other men in song and prayer as they awaited their deaths. Earlier in his life, Maximilian had lived in Japan and founded a monastery on the outskirts of Nagasaki. Four years after his martyrdom, on August 9, 1945, the atomic bomb was dropped on Nagasaki, but his monastery miraculously survived. Maximilian's feast day, when Christians around the world celebrate his life and sainthood as a hero of the church, falls during the week after Nagasaki Day. Each year, we spend that week reflecting on the best and the worst that human beings are capable of.

August 16: Solidarity in Poland. In 1989, a Solidarity-led government was elected in Poland, marking the beginning of a nonviolent victory over communism in Eastern Europe.

August 21: Nat Turner's Slave Revolt. In 1831, Nat Turner led a slave revolt in Southampton County, Virginia, killing fifty-five whites on his march to the county seat of Jerusalem, where he declared that the "great day of judgment" was at hand.

August 26: Women's Suffrage. In 1920, the United States Congress ratified the nineteenth amendment to the Constitution, guaranteeing women the right to vote.

August 28: Augustine of Hippo (354 – 430). One of the greatest influences on the theology of Western Christianity, Augustine wanted from a young age to understand the meaning of life and the nature of good and evil. As a teacher, he sought this understanding through the best philosophy of his day. Although his mother, Monica, had instructed him in the Christian faith, he was not drawn to the tradition, but later he found a depth and wisdom in Christianity capable of explaining evil and good. The famous story of Augustine's conversion involves an experience in a garden in Milan. Torn between living a life of chastity and remembering his former life of sin, he prayed for forgiveness and immediately heard the voice of a child singing from a neighboring house, "Take up and read!" He picked up a book of St. Paul's epistles which had been left nearby, and the words he found there changed him forever. After his baptism, Augustine moved to North Africa to pursue a monastic life, but at the urging of the church, he was ordained and later was made bishop of Hippo, where he served for thirty-five years. Augustine has rightly been criticized for silencing some important voices in his day and passing on a harmful view of the body. He was not perfect, but he himself insisted that grace is the heart of our faith.

August 29: John the Baptist (c. 30). John the Baptist was the son of Zechariah, a priest in the Jerusalem temple, and Elizabeth, a cousin of Mary, the mother of Jesus. John's parents were advanced in years and had prayed to have a child, yet had not conceived. But an angel of the Lord appeared to Zechariah and told him his wife would bear a son named John, "great in the sight of the Lord" and "filled with the Holy Spirit." Five months later, the same angel appeared to Mary and told her of the coming birth of Jesus. When Mary visited her cousin Elizabeth, Elizabeth's "baby leaped in her womb," a prophetic sign that John would be filled with the Holy Spirit all of his life. John lived in the wilderness of Judea until he was thirty, then began his public career preaching repentance. When Jesus came to him to be baptized, John recognized him as the Messiah and said, "It is I who need to be baptized by you." John often is referred to as the Precursor to Jesus; he foretold the coming of the Messiah and prepared the way for Jesus. His preaching encouraged many believers to follow Christ; in fact, Andrew and John learned of Christ through John's ministry.

August 30: Mississippi Freedom Democratic Party.
In 1964, Fannie Lou Hamer and Ruby D. Robinson led the Mississippi Freedom Democratic Party in its campaign to be seated at the Democratic National Convention, saying that they and thousands of African-Americans like them were "sick and tired of being sick and tired."

September 8: United Farm Workers Union. In 1965, Filipino and Mexican farmworkers in Delano, California, went on strike, leading to the founding of the United Farm Workers Union.

September 9: Peter Claver (1580 – 1654). The patron saint of slaves and African-Americans, Peter Claver was a Jesuit priest who served the church in seventeenth-century Cartagena, Colombia. During his ministry, as many as ten thousand African slaves came through the port of Cartagena each year. Recognizing the blasphemy of human slavery, Claver worked tirelessly in ministry among the slaves, baptizing and preaching to as many as three hundred thousand in his lifetime. After welcoming them into the church in a society that considered itself Christian, Claver advocated for slaves' legal rights as fellow Christians.

September 10: Mother Teresa of Calcutta (1910 – 1997).
Mother Teresa was born Agnesë Gonxhe Bojaxhiu in Albania. She joined the Sisters of Loreto, a Catholic religious order, at eighteen. After years of prayer and monastic discipline, she heard a "call within the call" to minister to Christ among the poorest of the poor in Calcutta, India. Moved with compassion for people

who were dying in the streets, Mother Teresa took them in and gave them basic care. With no resources or established programs, she begged for food and supplies to care for those she welcomed. When others came to help her, she started the Missionaries of Charity in 1950. For nearly half a century, she committed herself, and the movement she led, to serving Christ in his most distressing disguise among the poor, the sick, the orphaned, and the dying.

September 11: 1973 Chilean Coup/2001 Terrorist Attacks. On this day in 1973, the democratically elected government of Salvador Allende was overthrown in Chile by a CIA-backed coup. On the same day in 2001, terrorist attacks on the World Trade Center and the United States Pentagon killed more than twenty-eight hundred people.

September 12: Armenian Genocide in Turkey. In 1915, the genocide of Armenians in Turkey began, the first of four acts of genocide that plagued the twentieth century.

September 13: Attica Prison Revolt/Oslo Accords. In 1971, inmates at Attica Prison in New York revolted and took control of the facility, presenting a list of demands to the governor of New York that included removal of the warden, better living conditions, and amnesty for those who had participated in the uprising. On September 13, a combined military and police force stormed the prison. By the end of the day, thirty-one prisoners and nine prison guards were dead. As we remember the prisoners and guards who died at Attica, we also are mindful of the fact that more than 1 percent of the US population is incarcerated today. Also noteworthy are the Oslo Accords signed on September 13, 1993, a milestone in the ongoing conflict in the Middle East. They were the first face-to-face agreements between the government of Israel and the Palestine Liberation Organization, and were intended to be a framework for ongoing relations and negotiations in this troubled area of the Holy Land.

September 14: John Chrysostom (c. 347 – 407). As a young man, John Chrysostom tried to be a desert monk, but he was deterred by poor health. So he decided to give his whole life to God in the city. He eventually became archbishop of Constantinople, but always insisted on living a life of simplicity. John is remembered for his eloquence in preaching, especially against abuses of authority by both ecclesiastical and political leaders. After his death, he was given the Greek surname *Chrysostomos*, which means "golden-mouthed," because of his eloquence. John reminds us that in a time filled with so many words, words of truth have power to convict and transform.

September 15: Bombing of Sixteenth Street Baptist Church. On September 15, 1963, a man later identified as Robert Chambliss placed a bomb under the steps of Sixteenth Street Baptist Church in Birmingham, Alabama. Addie Mae Collins (14), Carole Robertson (14), Cynthia Wesley (14), and Denise McNair (11) were killed by the explosion, and twenty-two others were injured. The girls were attending Sunday school classes at the church. Chambliss was found not guilty of murder, but was given a hundred-dollar fine and six months in jail for possessing dynamite. He was retried in 1973 and received a life sentence for the bombing.

September 17: Hildegard of Bingen (1098 – 1179). Hildegard was sent to the convent at the age of eight, where she learned to read Scripture, pray, and chant. Even as a child, she experienced supernatural religious visions in which she saw things that were invisible to others, foretold the future, and was filled with a luminosity she later called "the reflection of the Living Light." At age thirty-eight, she became abbess of the Benedictine community in which she was raised and, five years later, received her call to prophesy when she saw a fiery light that infused her heart and mind with knowledge. She finally was able to understand her visions as a means of divine revelation and began to write extensively about them. Her term for the grace of God inherent in all living things was *viriditas*, or greenness, endearing her to followers of creation spirituality today. Hildegard's holistic approach to God and humanity is still relevant, particularly to those longing for the wholeness and healing of all of creation.

September 20: Paul Chong Hasang (1794? – 1839) and the Korean Martyrs. Paul Chon Hasang was the son of Augustine Chong Yak-jong, one of Korea's first converts to Christianity. When Paul's father and older brother were martyred, Paul's mother and remaining siblings, along with seven-year-old Paul, were spared. Paul became a government interpreter, which allowed him to travel and eventually meet a bishop in Beijing whom he entreated to send priests as missionaries to Korea. Years later, Paul learned Latin and theology, and he was about to be ordained when persecution broke out in 1839. Refusing to renounce his faith, Paul was bound to a cross on a cart. We remember him on this day, along with Andrew Kim Taegon, the first Korean-born Catholic priest, and 103 other Korean Christians who were martyred.

September 21: Henri Nouwen (1932 – 1996). Henri Nouwen was a Dutch Catholic priest who became an esteemed professor at both Yale and Harvard, but then followed the path of "downward mobility" in his pursuit of Jesus. He left the public eye to work among those struggling to survive in Latin America and then joined the work of L'Arche Daybreak Community in Canada. He was a "wounded healer" whose restless seeking for God left a legacy to the world through his prolific writings on the spirituality of brokenness and vulnerability. He died suddenly on this day in 1996.

September 27: Vincent de Paul (1581 – 1660). The son of French peasants, Vincent de Paul studied for the priesthood and was ordained in 1600. While serving the church, he was kidnapped by Turkish pirates and sold into slavery. After converting his master, Vincent escaped and returned to France, where he ministered to the poor and imprisoned, and invited others to join him, founding the Vincentians and the Daughters of Charity with Louise de Marillac. He prayed, "May the poor forgive me the bread that I give them."

October 1: Therese of Lisieux (1873 – 1897). Therese was born to a middle-class family in Lisieux, France. When she was fifteen, she got special permission to join her two older sisters at the Carmelite monastery in their hometown. When she died of tuberculosis nine years later at the age of twenty-four, she was little known outside her community. However, she had written, at the request of her spiritual director, a memoir of her spiritual journey, titled *The Story of a Soul*, which became a classic almost immediately for its powerfully clear articulation of one ordinary person's desire to give her whole life to Christ by following every moment in the "Little Way" of love and service to one's neighbors. "After my death," Therese wrote, "I will let fall a shower of roses. I will spend my heaven in doing good upon earth."

October 4: Francis of Assisi (1182 – 1226). Francis was born to a merchant family in the Italian city of Assisi. As a young man, he was attracted to adventure and moved by romantic tales of knights. When he himself became a knight, Francis met a leper while riding through the countryside. Overwhelmed by a divine impulse, Francis dismounted his horse, shared his coat with the leper, and kissed the man's diseased face. Captivated by the experience, Francis began to reimagine his life in light of the gospel, renouncing his selfish desires and his father's wealth. A beggar for Christ's sake, Francis inspired thousands to walk away from worldly success and join his movement of friars who sought to renew the church in their day.

October 6: Fannie Lou Hamer (1917 – 1977). Fannie Lou Hamer was born the daughter of sharecroppers in Mississippi, a poor black woman in the poorest region of America at the time. She rose from obscurity to challenge the principalities and powers of her day. A fiery and eloquent voice for freedom, she helped to guide and inspire the struggle for freedom. In Hamer's later years, her concerns grew beyond civil rights to include opposition to the Vietnam War and efforts to unite poor people of all shades of skin in a movement to end poverty. She was known for her line, "I am sick and tired of being sick and tired."

October 7: Afghan War. In 2001, a US-led coalition began bombing Afghanistan in response to the September 11 terrorist attacks.

October 9: Oskar Schindler (1908 – 1974). Oskar Schindler was a German living in Czechoslovakia when he joined the Nazi party in 1939. When Germany invaded Poland later that same year, he moved to Krakow and took over two manufacturing companies and, like many other businessmen there, made his fortune using cheap labor — Jews from the Krakow ghetto. When he witnessed the Germans deporting and killing Jews, Oskar was moved to transfer the Jewish workers from his factory to a safe place. Later, he received permission from the Germans to move not only his workers but other Jews as well to his native land of Czechoslovakia. Over time, Schindler's occupation changed, as rescuing Jews became his top priority. Using the factory as cover, he saved more and more Jews, putting his life in danger to insure the safety of those in his protection. At one point, when a train carrying more than one thousand Jews was on its way to a new factory site in Czechoslovakia, it was accidentally diverted to Auschwitz. Schindler offered the Nazis diamonds and gold to make sure those in his care reached safety. Ultimately, Schindler saved twelve hundred Jews from extermination, and today there are more than seven thousand descendants of the Schindler Jews living all over the world. Through his actions, Schindler was a living example of human decency, love, goodness, and compassion in the face of unspeakable horror. He has been called an unlikely hero, not only because nothing in his prior life suggested he would perform such heroic deeds to the extent that he did but also because he was an ordinary man who did extraordinary things. His life is a testament to the fact that we are all called to put our faith into action, sometimes in the most unexpected, bold, and courageous ways.

October 10: Women in Black. In 1991, the Women in Black began their regular Wednesday vigil against war in Belgrade, Serbia.

October 12: "Indigenous Peoples Day." In 1492, the indigenous peoples of the Americas discovered Christopher Columbus.

October 15: Teresa of Avila (1515 – 1582). In sixteenth-century Spain, where women had little voice, Teresa of Avila stood out as a spiritual giant, reforming her Carmelite order, founding seventeen new communities, writing four books, and challenging countless men and women to grow in the life of prayer. As attested to by her writings and by her friends and disciples (including John of the Cross), Teresa's own prayer life was perhaps her most important gift to the church. "Prayer," she wrote, "is nothing but friendly intercourse, and frequent solitary converse, with Him who we know loves us."

October 16: Cuban Missile Crisis. The Soviet Union and Cuba made an agreement in 1962 to allow the storage of nuclear missiles on the island of Cuba. Once the United States discovered the plan, the US Navy surrounded the island on October 16. Tensions were high as the Cold War enemies faced off ninety miles from US soil. The Soviet Union agreed to remove the missiles if the US removed its own missiles from southern Italy and Turkey and did not attack Cuba.

October 17: Ignatius of Antioch (c. 107). Ignatius, whose surname was Theophorus ("God-bearer"), may have been a disciple of John the Evangelist. Little is known about his early life, but he took charge of the church at Antioch around the year 69 and was condemned to death during the time of Trajan's persecution. While in transit to Rome, the boat carrying him to his death made stops along the shores of Asia Minor, and he was able to preach in the churches along the way. Faithful

Christians met Ignatius upon his arrival in Rome, both to celebrate his presence and mourn his impending death. Praying with the believers, he asked for an end to persecution, blessings on the church, and charity for the faithful. He was taken to the amphitheater in Rome, where, it was reported, two lions were set upon him.

October 19: John Woolman (1720 – 1772). John Woolman was born October 19, 1720. After refusing as a young man to write a bill of sale for a slave, Woolman went on to play a key role in challenging Quakers to give up slavery and recognize it as unchristian. Thanks to the active faith of Woolman and others, Quakers played an important role in the abolitionist movement throughout the nineteenth century.

October 29: Clarence Jordan (1912 – 1969). A son of the American South, Clarence Jordan was troubled by his people's comfortable embrace of both Jesus and racism. After studying for a doctorate in New Testament at the Southern Baptist Seminary, Jordan and his family returned to Georgia in 1942 to start Koinonia Farm, an interracial community in the heart of the Jim Crow South. Greeted by Ku Klux Klan members who told him, "Around here, we don't let the sun set on people like you," Jordan smiled and replied, "Pleased to meet ya'll. I've been waiting all my life to meet someone who could make the sun stand still."

November 1: All Saints. Since its earliest centuries, the church has set aside a day to remember the great cloud of witnesses who have gone before us in the faith, stretching across the centuries and around the globe. However hard it might seem to follow the way of Jesus in our own time and place, this is a day to remember that we may be crazy, but we are not alone.

November 2: World Christian Gathering of Indigenous People. In 1996, the first World Christian Gathering of Indigenous People took place in Rotorua, New Zealand. Founded by a Maori couple, Monte and Linda Ohia, the World Christian

Gathering is a coming together of the world's indigenous peoples to worship the Creator and celebrate their traditional cultures.

November 3: Martin de Porres. The illegitimate son of a Spanish nobleman in sixteenth-century Peru, Martin de Porres bore the complexion of his black mother. At fifteen, he presented himself to a Dominican monastery as someone who could sweep the floors, but his talents, especially in the art of healing, were soon recognized. As head of the monastery's infirmary, Martin not only treated the brothers but went out into the streets of Peru and brought in the poor, even offering his own bed for them to sleep in. When Martin was made a saint in 1962, Pope John XXIII named him patron of all who work for social justice.

November 4: Watchman Nee (1903 – 1972). Watchman Nee was a Chinese church leader in the early twentieth century. He was born into a Methodist family on November 4, 1903. Nee was a courageous pastor and writer who saw a great revival in China. He had no formal theological training, but with a deep commitment, he undertook thirty years of ministry in the underground church in China. Eventually, he was imprisoned for his faith and remained in prison for two decades until his death in 1972.

November 9: Fall of the Berlin Wall. In 1989, the Berlin Wall fell, signaling an end to the Cold War and a victory for the long nonviolent resistance to communism in Eastern Europe.

November 10: Kristallnacht. On November 10, 1938, Jewish men and women in Germany were beaten and murdered by Nazi troops. Jewish shops were destroyed and hundreds of synagogues were burned, their broken windows giving the evening its name — Kristallnacht, "the night of glass." Some twenty-five thousand Jewish men were sent to concentration camps. Following the brutality, Jewish people were forced to clean up the debris and were banned from all hospitals.

November 11: Armistice Day. Originally called Armistice Day, November 11 (Veteran's Day) is set aside to remember the 24.9 million military veterans in the United States.

November 22: Eberhard and Emmy Arnold (1883 – 1935; 1884 – 1980). During the Reformation, there were those who believed that Luther and Calvin did not go far enough in recovering the radical spirit of Christianity, namely in regard to the Christian attitude toward violence and personal property. These Radical Reformers stressed community, simplicity, and an uncompromising commitment to gospel nonviolence. They suffered persecution from Protestants and Catholics alike, and their spirit took root in such communities as the Hutterites and Mennonites, which continue to this day. Eberhard and Emmy Arnold drew on this tradition centuries later in the midst of Nazi Germany. They started a community called the Bruderhof ("house of brothers"), whose ethic was the Sermon on the Mount. Their presence was a prophetic critique of the nationalism and militarism of Nazi Germany and to the Christianity that was silent amid such evil. In November 1933, their community was taken over by the Gestapo and they fled. Eberhard died in 1935, but Emmy lived for forty-five more years, helping to start many other communities. Their lives and writings have inspired many communities, and their witness has touched people around the world.

November 26: Sojourner Truth. Sojourner Truth, named Isabella by her master, escaped from slavery to freedom in 1826 and worked for several years as a domestic in New York City. But when she heard a call to travel, going "up and down the land, showing the people their sins and being a sign unto them," Isabella changed her name and became an itinerant evangelist for the causes of abolition and women's rights. In 1864, she traveled to Washington, D.C., to encourage Abraham Lincoln in his struggle against the Confederacy, staying on to minister to the former slaves who had gathered in refugee camps. She was still there on December 12, 1865, when Congress ratified the thirteenth amendment to the Constitution, abolishing slavery in the United States.

November 29: Dorothy Day (1897 – 1980). Dorothy Day was born in Brooklyn in 1897. She worked as a journalist for radical newspapers in the 1920s and found most of her friends in the bohemian crowds that gathered in Greenwich Village. While living with a man she loved in 1926, she became pregnant and experienced a mysterious conversion to Jesus. As a Roman Catholic, she struggled to unite her personal faith with passion for social justice until she met Peter Maurin, with whom she founded the Catholic Worker Movement in 1933. Through hospitality houses in the city, agronomic universities on the land, and roundtable discussions for the clarification of thought, they aimed to "create a new society within the shell of the old," offering American Christianity the witness of a new monasticism that combines piety and practice, charity and justice.

FREQUENTLY ASKED QUESTIONS

Doesn't God want to hear the prayers of our heart? Why should I learn and say prayers written by other people?

Yes, Scripture says that the Holy Spirit empowers people who find new life in Christ to cry, "Abba." This is intimate language, the sort of language kids use for their parents. God isn't just willing to hear us. When we cry out in the Spirit, God hears the voice of the one who said, "I and the Father are one."

And yet, as intimate and personal as this communication is, it is never private. To be "in Christ" is to be part of a body that has prayed across the centuries and is now praying around the world. To pray in the Spirit is to join the eternal song of all the saints who sing around the throne of God. Because over time some of those prayers and songs have been written down, we do well to hide them in our hearts and make them our own.

Why do I need set prayers for different times of the day? Can't I just pray the prayers I need when I need them?

"Fixed hour prayer," the tradition of praying the hours — or saying particular prayers at specific times of day — is a practice that goes all the way back to ancient Judaism. Early Christianity picked this up because the church knew that it was called to live as a contrast society in the world. A regular rhythm of rooting ourselves in God's realm and God's time is a constant reminder that we are in the world but not of it. Fixed hour prayer regularly interrupts our schedules to remind us that the world has been interrupted by the kingdom of God and that we are called to be holy interruptions where we are.

I've heard of *The Book of Common Prayer*. Why a new *Common Prayer*? What's the point of a new prayer book? How is this one different?

If you are familiar with the Church of England's *Book of Common Prayer* (BCP), you'll recognize much of the language and rhythms of this prayer book. The BCP is the most beautiful and enduring prayer book in the English language, and we borrowed from it extensively. But we didn't feel too bad when we realized how much the BCP had borrowed from the Benedictine manuals of prayer that preceded it. Common prayer is a long tradition, and each new resource can only build on those that have come before it.

But *Common Prayer* also seeks to bring this tradition alive and make it dance in the here and now. It is, for one, accessible to people who have little experience with liturgical prayer. It also aims to draw in the gifts of the Pentecostals and the Baptists, the evangelicals and the black church traditions. Finally, *Common Prayer* is explicit about taking the liturgy to the streets — integrating our prayer and our action — by holding church time and its celebrations alongside the highs and lows of the struggle for justice and peace in our world.

Can I use this book for my personal devotions? Or is it just for groups to use together?

While *Common Prayer* is a liturgy designed to be said and sung together with other believers, the morning, midday, evening, and compline prayers in this pocket edition are arranged for easy personal use. Even when we are by ourselves, it's important to remember that we're not alone. These prayers are one way you can join your voice with others wherever you are.

If you are learning these prayers for your own use or for use with a group, we encourage you to learn how to sing the simple melodies to which many of these prayers have been set. Sheet music is available in the larger edition of *Common Prayer* and on the website *www.commonprayer.net*. You can also listen to a community saying and singing these prayers together on the audio version of *Common Prayer*, available on iTunes or at *www.audible.com*. For a short, video introduction to the morning office, visit *www.commonprayer.net/about*.

If these prayers are good news to you, we encourage you to find a group in your area that gathers to pray them regularly, or if you can't find one, invite a couple of friends and get one started at your church, in your office, on your cell block, or in your living room.

Who are "ordinary radicals"? Why is this liturgy for them?

Radical comes from the Latin word *radix*, which means "root." (It's also how we get our English word *radish*, which is a root vegetable, if you're not into gardening ...) Real radicals are people who get at the root of what something is really about. Ordinary radicals are folks who've heard the good news that getting at the root of the gospel and God's kingdom isn't just for the holy few; it's an adventure we're all invited into. When ordinary people in ordinary places begin to take Jesus at his word, their lives can suddenly seem radical. But this is what God's movement has always been about in the world.

Because not all radicals are Jesus radicals — just as not all extremists are extremists for love — we need resources to keep us rooted in God's story and God's life. That's what this liturgy is for. We discern what it means to follow Jesus with our whole lives here and now as we remember the saints who've gone before us, recall the story of God's people in Scripture, and pray the prayers that have led God's people in every generation.

Where can I learn more about the communities that *Common Prayer* grew out of?

Sometimes called a "new monasticism," there is a contemporary movement of ordinary radicals in North America that contributed songs, prayers, and stories of their communities to this project. You can learn more about The Simple Way (*www.thesimpleway.com*) and School for Conversion (*www.newmonasticism.org*), the organizations that facilitated this project, at their websites. You can also find a new monastic community near you via the online directory *www.communityofcommunities.info*.

We want to hear from you. Please send your comments about this
book to us in care of zreview@zondervan.com. Thank you.

ZONDERVAN.com/
AUTHORTRACKER
follow your favorite authors